THE
ICING
ON THE
CAKE

THE
ICING
ON THE
CAKE

YOUR ULTIMATE STEP-BY-STEP GUIDE TO DECORATING BAKED TREATS

Juliet Stallwood

DUNCAN BAIRD PUBLISHERS

LONDON

THE ICING ON THE CAKE
Juliet Stallwood

Distributed in the USA and Canada by
Sterling Publishing Co., Inc.
387 Park Avenue South
New York, NY 10016-8810

First published in the UK and USA in 2013 by
Duncan Baird Publishers, an imprint of
Watkins Publishing Limited
Sixth Floor
75 Wells Street
London W1T 3QH

A member of Osprey Group

Managing Editor: Grace Cheetham
Editors: Alison Bolus and Krissy Mallett
Art Direction and Design: Manisha Patel
Production: Uzma Taj
Commissioned Photography: Jon Whitaker
Food Stylist: Juliet Stallwood
Prop Stylist: Lucy Harvey

ISBN: 978-1-84899-082-1

10 9 8 7 6 5 4 3 2 1

Typeset in Century Old Style and Segoe Condensed
Color reproduction by XY Digital
Printed in China

For information about custom editions, special sales, premium and
corporate purchases, please contact Sterling Special Sales Department
at 800-805-5489 or specialsales@sterlingpub.com.

Publisher's note
While every care has been taken in compiling the recipes for this book,
Watkins Publishing Limited, or any other persons who have been involved
in working on this publication, cannot accept responsibility for any errors
or omissions, inadvertent or not, that may be found in the recipes or text,
nor for any problems that may arise as a result of preparing one of these
recipes. If you are pregnant or breastfeeding or have any special dietary
requirements or medical conditions, it is advisable to consult a medical
professional before following any of the recipes contained in this book.

Notes on the recipes
Unless otherwise stated:
Use fresh ingredients
1 tsp. = 5ml 1 tbsp. = 15ml 1 cup = 240ml

To make the most accurate and economical use of ingredients, and
to achieve the best results, use digital kitchen scales to weigh the gum
paste, flower paste and modeling paste called for in the recipes. Kitchen
scales are inexpensive and widely available online and in cookware stores.

DEDICATION
For my boys

Contents

Introduction

I am sitting writing this at an old pine table in the café of our village store in Dorset in South West England. My bakery is on the first floor, with its shiny worktops, ovens and racks. The window of the bakery looks out over our village primary school, church and my house, with the hills of the Cranbourne Chase in the distance. It's a very inspirational place in which to live, bake and decorate.

My family moved to Dorset from West Sussex, where I had been working as a graphic designer with my brother and his wife. It was here that our boys, now 15 and 13, were born. As they grew up I always looked forward to making their birthday cakes, and it was these early creations that sparked my love of cake decorating. I started out making novelty cakes, which I would base on the latest craze the children were into. Soon I started to get requests from friends and family for different, sometimes more challenging, cakes. I always felt that the last cake I had made was a bit better than the one before. I learned something new with each project and, even though I had only read about cake decorating, it seemed to come quite naturally to me.

Over the next few years, cake decorating continued to be a hobby that I thoroughly enjoyed. I loved the whole process—the designing, the baking and, of course, the decorating. However, I always received the most pleasure, and still do, from seeing the recipient's face or receiving a thank you email telling me how delighted they were. On moving to my village, I fitted making cakes for family and friends around other commitments. I was working less as a freelance graphic designer and started to bake more and more. My involvement with the primary school meant I could hold more bake sales— always a winner on the playground. I used these sales to apply techniques that I had learned from my party-pleasing novelty cakes to smaller cupcakes. I am always excited by the opportunity to try out new ideas. Even now, as soon as a friend mentions they are holding an event, from a wedding to a tea party, I jump in there and ask if I can be of any help, or to put it plainly, "Can I make you a cake?"

As my cakes became more sophisticated, I started to pay more and more attention to detail. In the fall of 2010, I saw a picture of some cookies that had been iced in a highly decorative style. I had never seen anything like them before, and knew I had to try the technique for myself. An opportunity presented itself when I went to a meeting at my sons' school to discuss its forthcoming Christmas Market. Without even thinking, I volunteered to take on a stand selling iced cookies.

Having taken the plunge, I started thinking about what I was actually going to make. I also began dreaming about the image I wanted to project to the customers I hoped would come flocking to my stand. I didn't want them to think that I had just made a few cookies to sell at the fair, and that was that. I wanted them to understand that baking and decorating were things I was passionate about. Endless cookie making was coupled with designing decoration schemes on the computer. I experimented day after day and by the time the market came along, I had everything organized. One customer simply could not believe that just a few weeks previously I had never even baked a cookie before. This was the turning point when I decided that I wanted to turn my baking and decorating into a business.

The following months flew by as I spent hours sitting at the kitchen table drawing up ideas for Valentine's Day and Easter ranges. It was very early on in my new career, but I took the step of setting up a website (with a little help from my family), which increased my potential clientele. Cakes were tricky because they could only realistically be sold locally. Still, baking and decorating cakes continued in earnest, and also went hand in hand with other little treats, like macarons and fondant fancies. Cookies, on the other hand, opened the door to the world. They can be mailed anywhere, and over the next year I started to develop and refine my own techniques with every new design.

In the beginning, the books I read inspired me to practice and improve, and eventually to have the confidence to create my own designs and techniques. Baking and decorating presents endless possibilities. Nearly any image you can think of can be made into a cake or a cookie, from a ghost to a teapot and from a hen to a handbag. The designing is always exciting—a few quick sketches, a little color, a few embellishments, and there it is. The decorating process can often involve many stages, and patience is needed along with a steady hand. But once you see how each new project comes to life as the last spoonful of icing is added, I know you'll agree it's well worth the wait.

I love what I do and I love sharing my passion. I began running courses at the bakery so I could teach other enthusiasts the essential skills and techniques I have picked up along the way. This book is an extension of that goal—helping you to learn at your own pace, in your own time and in your own home.

Designs don't have to be complicated to look effective. In fact, the simplest ones are often the best. There are projects in this book for the decorating novice that are very quick and easy to do, and others that may take a little more time to master. In Chapter One, "Decorate to Indulge," you'll find lots of ideas for simple sweet treats for any day of the week. Chapter Two, "Decorate for Love," revels in the art of romance and includes inspiring ideas for occasions like weddings, anniversaries and Valentine's Day. Chapter Three, "Decorate to Celebrate," is full of treats to make birthday parties, baby showers and holiday festivities extra special. Chapter 4 is my *pièce de résistance*, "Decorate to Impress," where you'll discover how to make extravagant centerpieces that will amaze your family and friends.

Whatever your level of expertise, this book will help you bring out plate after plate of beautifully decorated goodies. It's the icing on the cake.

Juliet Stallwood

CHAPTER ONE

You don't have to wait for a special occasion to decorate sweet treats. With a little time and a few basic tools, you can easily turn a small family gathering on a Sunday afternoon or coffee with friends into something more indulgent. You could make something as simple as Chocolate-Dipped Florentines, as delicious as Decadent Fruit Tartlets or as stunning as the Rose Swirl Cupcakes. Go on! Have your cake and eat it.

DECORATE
TO
INDULGE

Sugared Rose Petal Cake

MAKES 1 CAKE
petals from 1–2 edible pink
or red roses
1 large egg white, lightly beaten
heaped ½ cup sugar
2 x 6in. round Vanilla Sponge
Cakes (see pages 62–3)
½ recipe quantity Vanilla
Buttercream (see page 16)

YOU WILL NEED
small paintbrush
baking sheet lined with
parchment paper
6in. round cake board

HINT
The crystallized rose petals can
be stored in an airtight container
lined with parchment paper up
to 1 week. Do not store in the
refrigerator or they will become
soggy.

1 Carefully separate the petals from the rose(s), taking care not to bruise them as you do so. Using the paintbrush, gently brush the petals to remove any debris. Discard any petals that are damaged or discolored. Transfer the petals to the prepared baking sheet.

2 Lightly brush the egg white over both sides of each petal with the paintbrush **(a)**, making sure they are completely coated—if sections of the petals remain uncoated, the sugar will not stick and you will be left with an uneven finish.

3 Pour the sugar into a bowl. Holding one of the petals over the bowl, gently sprinkle a little sugar over the petal with a teaspoon **(b)**, making sure it is completely coated. Shake off any excess sugar and return the petal to the prepared baking sheet. Repeat until all the petals are coated. Leave the petals to dry overnight, uncovered, at room temperature.

4 Following the instructions on page 150 and using the cake board as a firm base, layer the cakes, then fill with buttercream to make one tall cake. Following the instructions on page 152, cover the cake with the remaining buttercream. Chill in the refrigerator 2 hours.

5 When the buttercream has set and the petals have dried and become hard, carefully transfer the covered cake to a cake stand or serving plate and scatter with the petals.

(a)

(b)

Chocolate Swirl Mini Cupcakes

MAKES 24 CUPCAKES
1¾oz. semi-sweet chocolate
    confectionery coating
½ recipe quantity lilac-colored
    Vanilla Frosting (see page 118)
24 Chocolate Sponge Mini
    Cupcakes baked in foil mini
    baking cups (see page 129)
½ recipe quantity turquoise-
    colored Vanilla Frosting
    (see page 118)

YOU WILL NEED
chocolate swirl designs
    (see page 162)
8 x 11in. sheet of paper
parchment paper
pastry bag with a no. 2 plain tip
    attached
pastry bag with a ½in. open-star
    tip attached

HINT
Confectionery coating (also called candy coating) is widely available online. You can buy it in various colors and in a variety of flavors including dark, milk and white chocolate. Confectionery coating is easy to use because, unlike chocolate, it does not need to be tempered. Heating and cooling chocolate without controlling the temperature (tempering) causes blemishes to appear on the surface. The chocolate will also crumble rather than snap.

1 Trace 24 chocolate swirl designs onto the sheet of paper and lay a sheet of parchment paper on top **(a)**.

2 Put the confectionery coating in a heatproof bowl and rest it over a saucepan of gently simmering water, making sure the bottom of the bowl does not touch the water. Heat, stirring occasionally, until melted. Alternatively, put the coating in a bowl and microwave, uncovered, on medium 2 minutes until melted, stirring every 30 seconds to ensure the coating does not overheat. The confectionery coating should have a smooth pouring consistency similar to heavy cream.

3 Spoon the melted confectionery coating into the pastry bag with the no. 2 plain tip attached. Carefully pipe over the outline of each swirl **(b)** to make 24 chocolate swirls. (For hints on piping, see pages 157–9.) Set the chocolate swirls aside at least 10 minutes until the coating has completely set—you can transfer the chocolate swirls to the refrigerator to speed this process up, if you like.

4 Spoon the lilac frosting into the pastry bag with a ½in. open-star tip attached to it and pipe a high swirl onto half of the mini cupcakes (see page 157). Clean the pastry bag and repeat with the turquoise frosting until all of the mini cupcakes have been frosted with a swirl.

5 Gently lift one of the chocolate swirls from the parchment paper with a knife, handling it carefully because it will be very delicate. Place it on top of one of the frosted cupcakes, gently pressing it into the frosting with your finger. Repeat until all the mini cupcakes are topped with a chocolate swirl.

(a)

(b)

Basic Buttercream

MAKES 1LB. 2OZ.
heaped 2 cups powdered sugar
1 cup (2 sticks) salted butter,
    softened
food coloring pastes (optional)

YOU WILL NEED
electric mixer
toothpick (optional)

HINT
1 recipe quantity makes enough buttercream to cover an 8in. cake, 12 cupcakes or 24 mini cupcakes. (For quantities for filling and covering different cake sizes with buttercream, see page 155.)

Buttercreams help to keep cakes moist and are often used to fill and cover cakes before they are covered with gum paste. They can be made in a variety of flavors to complement different sponge cake recipes (see below). Plain, vanilla and citrus buttercreams can also be colored with food coloring pastes. To color, simply add a small amount of food coloring paste to the mixture using the end of a toothpick, and combine. Repeat until the desired color is achieved. (For hints on filling and covering cakes with buttercream, see pages 150 and 152.)

For basic buttercream, sift the powdered sugar into a mixing bowl. Add the butter and beat with the electric mixer 5 minutes until pale, light and fluffy.

Variations

Cappuccino Buttercream: beat in 2 tsp. (or more to taste) of coffee extract with the powdered sugar and butter.
Chocolate Buttercream: use heaped 1¾ cups powdered sugar and ¼ cup unsweetened cocoa powder, then beat together with the butter.
Citrus Buttercream: beat in the finely grated zest of 1 large lemon or 1 orange with the powdered sugar and butter.
Mocha Buttercream: use heaped 1¾ cups of powdered sugar, ¼ cup unsweetened cocoa powder and add 1 tsp. (or more to taste) of coffee extract.
Vanilla Buttercream: beat in 2 tsp. of vanilla extract with the powdered sugar and butter.

Chocolate Ganache

MAKES 1LB. 5OZ.
10½oz. baking chocolate, at
    least 53% cocoa solids, broken
    into pieces, or chocolate chips
1¼ cups heavy cream

HINTS
If the mixture splits, warm up a little more cream, add it to the mixture and stir until smooth.

1 recipe quantity makes enough chocolate ganache to cover an 8in. cake or 12 cupcakes. (For quantities for covering different cake sizes with chocolate ganache, see page 155.)

1 Put the chocolate into a heatproof bowl. Rest the bowl over a saucepan of gently simmering water, making sure the bottom of the bowl does not touch the water. Heat, stirring occasionally, until melted. Alternatively, put the chocolate in a bowl and microwave, uncovered, on medium 2 minutes until melted, stirring every 30 seconds to ensure the chocolate does not burn.

2 Pour the cream into a saucepan over low heat and bring to a boil slowly. Pour the hot cream over the melted chocolate. Whisk until smooth and thickened, but take care not to overmix or the mixture will split.

3 Allow the ganache to cool 10 minutes, or until it is just starting to set, before using. Any leftover ganache can be stored in an airtight container in the refrigerator up to 1 month.

Use this buttercream recipe for the following recipes throughout this book:

**Sugared Rose
Petal Cake**
page 12

**Fresh Flower
Fondant Fancies**
page 18

Chocolate Fan Cake
page 30

Valentine Cigarillo Cake
page 48

**Chocolate Box Cake
with Truffles**
page 52

**Pom Pom
Wedding Cake**
page 60

Dragon Cake
page 74

**White Blossom
Christening Cake**
page 84

Mini Ghost Cakes
page 91

Festive Ball Cakes
page 92

**Christmas
Pudding Cake**
page 97

Butterfly Fancies
page 116

Teapot Cake
page 122

Rose Cupcakes
page 126

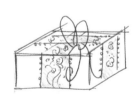

Gift-Wrapped Cake
page 135

Daisy Chain Mouse Cake
page 136

Use this chocolate ganache recipe for the following recipes throughout this book:

Chocolate Fan Cake
page 30

Ivory Corsage Wedding Cake
page 114

Fresh Flower Fondant Fancies

MAKES 16 FANCIES
7in. square Vanilla Sponge Cake
  (see pages 62–3), cooled
1 recipe quantity Vanilla Sugar
  Syrup (see page 119)
½ recipe quantity Vanilla
  Buttercream (see page 16)
2 heaped tbsp. seedless
  raspberry jam
powdered sugar, for dusting
6oz. marzipan
2 tbsp. apricot jam
4¾ cups dry fondant
ivory food coloring paste
lilac food coloring paste
16–20 fresh edible flowers,
  such as campanulas or violets

YOU WILL NEED
cake leveler or long serrated
  knife
pastry brush
metal spatula
rolling pin
¼in. marzipan spacers
  (optional)
sharp knife
icing smoother
ruler
long serrated knife
baking sheet lined with
  parchment paper
16 foil or paper baking cups
pastry bag

HINTS
If the marzipan sticks to the
rolling pin, dust the pin with
a little powdered sugar before
continuing to roll.

For the best results, cook the
vanilla sponge cake the day
before it is needed, then wrap
it in parchment paper and foil
and leave it to rest overnight to
firm up a little—this will make
it easier to cut.

1 Chill the cake in the refrigerator at least 1 hour until very cold and firm—this will make it easier to cut. Using the cake leveler, level the top of the cake, then slice it in half horizontally. Brush the cut side of each layer with sugar syrup, then spread a thin layer of buttercream over the top of one layer and a thin layer of raspberry jam over the other with the metal spatula. Carefully sandwich the two layers together, then seal the cake in plastic wrap and chill in the refrigerator at least 30 minutes, ideally 2 hours. (For hints on layering and filling cakes, see page 150.)

2 Meanwhile, dust the work surface with a little powdered sugar, then knead the marzipan until smooth. Roll out the kneaded marzipan until it is ¼in. thick, using marzipan spacers if you like, and cut out a square large enough to cover the top of the cake.

3 When the cake has chilled, remove from the refrigerator and remove the plastic wrap. Warm the apricot jam in a small saucepan over low heat, stirring occasionally, until it has a smooth, spreadable consistency. Alternatively, put the apricot jam in a small bowl and microwave, uncovered, on medium 20 seconds. Brush the top of the cake with a thin layer of the jam, then gently place the rolled marzipan on top of the cake, taking care not to stretch or pull it. Smooth the marzipan with your hands, then smooth again with the icing smoother to achieve a flat level surface.

4 Trim the sides of the cake and cut out a large square measuring 6¼ x 6¼in. Using the sharp knife, score the marzipan into 16 equal squares about 1½ x 1½in. each, then use the serrated knife to cut down through the marzipan and cake to make 16 small square cakes. Transfer the cakes to the prepared baking sheet, then cover with plastic wrap and leave to chill in the refrigerator until needed.

5 Make half of the fondant icing according to the package instructions in a deep heatproof bowl. Add a small amount of ivory food coloring paste and stir until thoroughly combined. Repeat until the desired color is achieved. Rest the bowl over a saucepan of gently simmering water until it has a smooth pouring consistency similar to heavy cream. Alternatively, put the dry fondant and water mixture into a bowl and microwave, uncovered, on medium 1 minute.

6 Remove half of the cakes from the refrigerator. Following the instructions on page 151, cover a cake in the ivory fondant and wrap in a baking cup, then leave to one side until the fondant has completely set. Repeat to make eight ivory fondant fancies in total. Repeat steps 5 and 6 with the remaining dry fondant, lilac food coloring paste and the remaining cakes to make 16 fondant fancies in total. Store any remaining fondant in an airtight container and leave to one side until needed—the icing will start to set as it cools.

7 When the fancies have set, spoon some of the remaining fondant into a pastry bag, and snip off the end if needed. Pipe a small dot of icing on top of each fancy and place an edible flower on top.

Sprinkle Whoopie Pies

MAKES 12 PIES
scant 1 cup superfine sugar
1 cup (2 sticks) salted butter,
    softened
1 large egg, beaten
scant 1¼ cups buttermilk
2 tsp. vanilla extract
1½ cups all-purpose flour
1 tsp. baking soda
heaped ½ cup unsweetened
    cocoa powder
1¾ cups powdered sugar
1 cup marshmallow creme
¼ cup white nonpareil sprinkles

YOU WILL NEED
electric mixer
1¾in. spring-action release
    ice-cream scoop (optional)
2 baking sheets lined with
    parchment paper, plus extra
    parchment paper for relining
    the baking sheets
metal spatula
pastry bag

1 Preheat the oven to 325°F. Put the sugar and ½ cup (1 stick) of the butter in a mixing bowl and beat with the electric mixer until light and fluffy. Gradually beat in the egg, followed by the buttermilk and 1 teaspoon of the vanilla extract. If the mixture starts to curdle, add a little bit of the flour. Sift the flour, baking soda and unsweetened cocoa powder into the bowl, then beat gently until just combined. Cover the bowl with plastic wrap and chill in the refrigerator 30 minutes until firm.

2 Working in batches, scoop out 12 golf ball-sized balls of the mixture with the ice cream scoop or a tablespoon and drop them onto the prepared baking sheets, spacing them about 2¼in. apart to allow each one to spread slightly during baking. Cover the remaining mixture with plastic wrap and return it to the refrigerator while you bake the first batch. Bake the prepared pies about 10 minutes or until the tops spring back slightly when gently pressed. Remove from the oven.

3 Without removing the sponge-cake halves, slide the sheets of parchment paper onto wire racks and leave to cool completely. Meanwhile, line the baking sheets with more parchment paper and repeat steps 2 and 3 with the remaining mixture.

4 To make the filling, sift the powdered sugar into a clean mixing bowl, then add the remaining vanilla extract and butter and beat with the electric mixer 2 minutes until smooth. Add the marshmallow creme, then beat about 3 minutes until light and fluffy.

5 Gently remove the sponge-cake halves from the parchment paper with the metal spatula. Spoon the filling into the pastry bag, then snip off ½in. from the tip if necessary. Pipe a flat swirl of filling onto the flat side of one sponge-cake half—starting from the edge and swirling the filling toward the center. Sandwich together the piped sponge-cake half with a plain sponge-cake half to make a whoopie pie.

6 Pour the nonpareil sprinkles into a small, shallow bowl. Holding the whoopie pie over the bowl, gently sprinkle the nonpareils over the edge of the filling with a teaspoon, turning the pie as you do so to ensure the filling is completely covered—if sections of the filling remain uncovered you will be left with an uneven finish. Shake off any excess and transfer the whoopie pie to a plate. Filling and decorating one whoopie pie at a time, repeat steps 5 and 6 with the remaining sponge-cake halves, filling and nonpareils until the edge of the filling of every pie is completely covered in nonpareil sprinkles.

Rose Swirl Cupcakes

MAKES 12 CUPCAKES
12 Chocolate Sponge Cake
  Cupcakes, baked in foil baking
  cups (see page 129)
1 recipe quantity pale pink-
  colored Basic Frosting (see
  page 118)

YOU WILL NEED
small serrated knife
pastry bag with a large closed-
  star tip attached
12 paper lollipop sticks about
  6in. long
vase and fresh foliage (optional)
pieces of ribbon (optional)

HINTS
To achieve a roselike effect, you
need to keep the swirl as flat as
possible, so try not to overlap the
frosting as you pipe.

Do not pour water in the vase
if using real foliage because the
paper lollipop sticks will get soggy
and no longer support
the cupcakes.

1 Using the serrated knife, trim off the domed top of each cupcake to create a level surface.

2 Spoon the frosting into the pastry bag. Pipe a flat swirl (see page 157) over each cupcake—starting from the center of the cupcake **(a)** and swirling the frosting around the edge **(b)**. (For hints on piping, see pages 157–9.)

3 Pierce a hole in the center of each cupcake base with a skewer, pushing it through the foil baking cup and about 1in. into the cake. Insert one of the lollipop sticks into each hole, then place the cakes in a vase with some fresh foliage to create a bouquet centerpiece, if you like. Alternatively, decorate each cupcake stick with a piece of ribbon.

(a)

(b)

Gingerbread Family

MAKES 12 COOKIES
powdered sugar, for dusting
1¾oz. brightly colored gum paste in one or more colors (see pages 160–1)
½ cup white soft-peak Royal Icing (see page 46)
12 cookies made using 1 recipe quantity Gingerbread Cookie Dough (see page 27), cut out with the gingerbread family templates (see page 163)
edible glue (optional)
edible glitter (optional)

YOU WILL NEED
small rolling pin
⅝in. and ½in. circle cutters
toothpick
metal spatula
baking sheet lined with parchment paper
pastry bag with a no. 2 plain tip attached
small paintbrush (optional)

HINTS
If you do not have a ½in. circle cutter, use the flat top of a pencil, covered in a tiny piece of plastic wrap, to indent the buttons.

You will need to make the buttons at least a day before they are needed. Try making flower- or heart-shaped buttons instead, if you like.

1 Dust the work surface with a little powdered sugar, then knead the gum paste(s) until soft and pliable. Roll out the kneaded gum paste(s) quite thinly. To make the buttons, stamp out 2 circles per large cookie and 1 circle per small cookie with the ⅝in. circle cutter.

2 While the gum paste buttons are still soft, position the ½in. circle cutter over the center of each one and gently press it down to indent a circle into the buttons **(a)**. Do not cut through the gum paste completely. Using the toothpick, punch 4 holes into the center of each indented circle to create a button effect **(b)**. Using the metal spatula, carefully transfer the gum-paste buttons to the prepared baking sheet. Leave them to dry overnight, uncovered, in a cool, dry place.

3 When the buttons have dried, spoon the royal icing into the pastry bag. Pipe a gingerbread person outline onto the top of each gingerbread person, then pipe a face onto each one. You can also pipe items of clothing onto the cookies, if you like (see picture). To attach the buttons, pipe small dots of icing onto the center of the cookies, then place a gum-paste button on top. Leave the cookies at least 30 minutes in a cool, dry place, to allow the royal icing to set.

It's easy to add a little glamor to your gingerbread family. Simply leave the dried gum-paste buttons on the prepared baking sheet and brush each one with a little edible glue. Dip the end of a teaspoon in edible glitter, then holding the spoon in one hand, gently tap the handle with the other to lightly dust the buttons with glitter. (For tips on dusting decorations with glitter see page 45). Repeat until all of the buttons are glittered. Pour any excess glitter on the parchment paper back into the pot. Wait until the edible glue is completely dry before attaching the gum paste buttons as above.

(a)

(b)

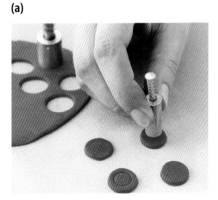
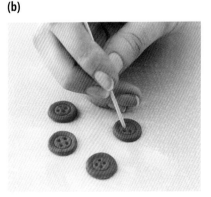

Basic Cookies

**MAKES ABOUT
30 COOKIES**
**1 cup (2 sticks) salted butter,
softened**
scant 1 cup superfine sugar
1 large egg, lightly beaten
3⅔ cups all-purpose flour

YOU WILL NEED
electric mixer
rolling pin
metal spatula
**2 baking sheets lined
with parchment paper**

1 Put the butter and sugar in a mixing bowl and beat with the electric mixer until the mixture is just pale and fluffy. Add the egg and beat until combined. Sift the flour into the bowl and mix with a wooden spoon until just combined.

2 Preheat the oven to 350°F. Roll out the cookie dough and cut out your cookies following the instructions on page 148. Tightly seal any leftover dough in plastic wrap and store in the refrigerator up to 1 week or freeze up to 3 months. Using the metal spatula, transfer the cookies to the prepared baking sheets, spacing them 1¼in. apart to allow each one to spread slightly during baking.

3 Bake the cookies 8 minutes, or until golden brown, then remove from the oven. Using the metal spatula, transfer the cookies to a wire rack and leave to cool completely. If not decorating the cookies immediately, store in an airtight container until needed.

Variations
Almond Cookies: beat in 1 tsp. almond extract with the butter and sugar.
Chocolate Cookies: use 3 cups all-purpose flour and scant ⅔ cup unsweetened cocoa powder.
Citrus Cookies: beat in the finely grated zest of 1 lemon or 1 orange with the butter and sugar.
Vanilla Cookies: beat in 1 tsp. vanilla extract with the butter and sugar.

Use this cookie recipe for the following recipes throughout this book:

Kissing Birds Cookies
page 42

Glitter Filigree Cookies
page 45

Corset Cookies
page 50

**Wedding Favor
Blossom Cookies**
page 58

Rose Heart Cookies
page 64

**Christmas Wreath
Tree Decorations**
page 72

Thanksgiving Cookies
page 83

Easter Hen Cookies
page 99

Mother's Day Cookies
page 100

Gingerbread Cookies

**MAKES ABOUT
20 COOKIES**
½ cup soft brown sugar
2 tbsp. plus 1½ tsp. light corn
   syrup
2 tbsp. molasses
2 tbsp. ground ginger
2 tbsp. ground cinnamon
½ cup (1 stick) salted butter,
   chilled and diced
½ tsp. baking soda
2¼ cups all-purpose flour

YOU WILL NEED
rolling pin
metal spatula
2 baking sheets lined
   with parchment paper

1 Put the sugar, light corn syrup, molasses, ginger, cinnamon and 2 tablespoons water in a saucepan. Bring to a boil slowly over medium-high heat, stirring occasionally, until the mixture is gently bubbling. Remove the pan from the heat and add the butter. Stir until the butter has melted and the mixture is glossy and smooth, then stir in the baking soda. Pour the mixture into a large bowl and leave to cool 30 minutes. When the mixture has cooled, sift the flour into the bowl and mix with a wooden spoon until just combined.

2 Preheat the oven to 350˚F. Roll out the gingerbread dough and cut out your cookies, following the instructions on page 148. Tightly seal any leftover dough in plastic wrap and store in the refrigerator up to 1 week or freeze up to 3 months. Using the metal spatula, transfer the cookies to the prepared baking sheets, spacing them 1¼in. apart to allow them to spread slightly during cooking.

3 Bake the cookies 8 minutes, or until the edges of the cookies have darkened slightly, then remove from the oven. Using the metal spatula, transfer the cookies to a wire rack and leave to cool completely. If not decorating the cookies immediately, store in an airtight container until needed.

Use this gingerbread cookie recipe for the following recipes throughout this book:

Gingerbread Family
page 25

Kissing Birds Cookies
page 42

**Glitter Filigree
Cookies**
page 45

Corset Cookies
page 50

**Wedding Favor
Blossom Cookies**
page 58

Rose Heart Cookies
page 64

**Christmas Wreath
Tree Decorations**
page 72

Gingerbread House
page 78

Thanksgiving Cookies
page 83

Easter Hen Cookies
page 99

Mother's Day Cookies
page 100

Designer Mini Brownies

MAKES 30 MINI BROWNIES
1 scant cup (1¾ sticks) salted butter, diced
5½oz. dark chocolate
1¾oz. milk chocolate
1⅔ cups superfine sugar
3 large eggs
½ tsp. vanilla extract
1 cup all-purpose flour
½ tsp. baking powder
7oz. semi-sweet chocolate confectionery coating
chocolate transfer sheet

YOU WILL NEED
10 x 12in. baking pan lined with parchment paper, plus extra parchment paper for lining the transfer sheet (for hints on lining baking pans, see page 149)
ruler
metal spatula
sharp knife

HINT
Chocolate transfer sheets are acetate sheets embossed with cocoa butter and powdered food coloring. When melted chocolate is spread on top and left to set, the design is transferred onto the surface of the chocolate. Many different designs are available online. For beginners, it's easier to transfer designs onto melted chocolate confectionery coating, which does not need to be tempered and is also available in dark, milk and white chocolate flavors. Heating and cooling chocolate without controlling the temperature (tempering) causes blemishes to appear on the surface. The chocolate will also crumble rather than snap. If you're a confident baker and decorator, try transferring the design onto tempered chocolate.

1 Preheat the oven to 350°F. Melt the butter, dark chocolate and milk chocolate in a large saucepan over low heat, then remove the pan from the heat. Stir in the sugar, then slowly beat in the eggs, one at a time. Stir in the vanilla extract, then sift the flour and baking powder into the bowl. Fold the flour and baking powder into the mixture with a metal spoon until thoroughly combined and smooth.

2 Pour the mixture into the prepared pan, leveling the surface with the back of a spoon. Bake 30 to 35 minutes, or until the surface is cracked and a skewer inserted into the center comes out clean. Take care not to overcook the brownies or they will dry out and loose their soft, dense center. Remove from the oven and leave in the pan to cool completely.

3 To give your brownies a designer finish, put 6oz. of the confectionery coating in a heatproof bowl and rest it over a saucepan of gently simmering water, making sure the bottom of the bowl does not touch the water. Heat, stirring occasionally, until melted. Alternatively, put the confectionery coating in a bowl and microwave, uncovered, on medium 2 minutes until melted, stirring every 30 seconds to ensure the coating does not overheat. The confectionery coating should have a smooth pouring consistency similar to heavy cream.

4 Cut the chocolate transfer sheet into a 10 x 12in. rectangle, then cut out a sheet of parchment paper or foil that is slightly larger than the transfer sheet. Put the sheet of parchment paper on the work surface and lay the chocolate transfer sheet, embossed-side up, over the top. Spoon the melted confectionery coating onto the transfer sheet and use the metal spatula to spread it into as thin and even a layer as possible. Leave to semi-set about 5 minutes, or until the surface of the melted confectionery coating loses its shiny appearance.

5 Using the sharp knife, cut through the confectionery coating and transfer sheet to form thirty 2 x 2in. squares. If you find the knife is dragging through the confectionery coating as you cut, leave it to set another minute or so, then try again. Carefully put the candy-coated transfer sheet squares in the refrigerator and leave to chill 20 minutes or until the confectionery coating has completely set. Make sure that the squares are kept flat.

6 Meanwhile, cut the brownies into thirty 2 x 2in. squares. When the transfer sheet squares have completely set, use the sharp knife to gently ease the squares away from the acetate. Melt the remaining confectionery coating as above in step 3. Spread a little melted confectionery coating over the surface of each brownie and place a transfer sheet decoration over the top.

Chocolate Fan Cake

MAKES 1 CAKE
powdered sugar, for dusting
¾oz. milk modeling chocolate
¾oz. dark modeling chocolate
2 x 6in. round Rich Chocolate
    Cakes (see pages 56–7)
½ recipe quantity Chocolate
    Buttercream (see page 16)
½ recipe quantity Chocolate
    Ganache (see page 16)

YOU WILL NEED
small rolling pin
sharp knife
ruler
baking sheet lined with
    parchment paper
6in. round cake board

HINT
Using a metal spatula to cover the
cake with ganache will produce an
attractively textured finish.

1 Dust the work surface with a little powdered sugar, then knead the milk modeling chocolate until it is soft and pliable. Roll out the kneaded modeling chocolate quite thinly and cut out 3 rectangles, each about 2 x 3½in. **(a)**, rerolling the modeling paste for the third rectangle, if necessary.

2 Gently concertina each rectangle, pinching the folds together at the base to form a fan **(b)**. Using the sharp knife, cut off any excess modeling chocolate at the base of the fans to neaten the edges **(c)**. Repeat steps 1 and 2 with the dark modeling chocolate to make six fans in total. Transfer the fans to the prepared baking sheet and leave to set a few hours or overnight, uncovered, in a cool, dry place.

3 When the fans have dried, following the instructions on page 150 and using the cake board as a firm base, layer the chocolate cakes, then fill them with chocolate buttercream to make one tall cake. Following the instructions on page 152, cover the cake with chocolate ganache. Chill in the refrigerator 2 hours.

4 When the ganache has set, arrange the chocolate fans on top of the cake, gently pressing them into the ganache to hold them in place.

(a)   **(b)**   **(c)**

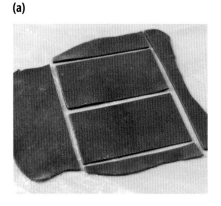
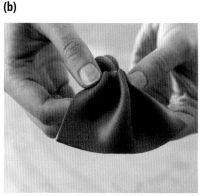

Decadent Fruit Tartlets

MAKES 12 TARTLETS
1½oz. caramel gum paste
   (see pages 160–1)
½ cup powdered sugar, sifted,
   plus extra for dusting
scant ⅓ cup ground almonds
½ cup (1 stick) chilled salted
   butter, diced, plus extra for
   greasing
heaped 1½ cups all-purpose
   flour
5 large egg yolks
heaped ¼ cup superfine sugar
¼ tsp. vanilla extract
generous 1 cup whole milk
gold edible lustre dust
1⅓ cups fresh fruit, such as
   raspberries, blueberries and
   blackberries

YOU WILL NEED
rolling pin
1in. veined leaf plunger cutter
indented foam pad or a piece
   of crinkled aluminum foil
12-cup muffin pan
parchment paper
¼in. marzipan spacers
   (optional)
3½in. fluted round cookie cutter
ceramic baking beans
small paintbrush
pastry bag

HINT
Make the gold gum paste
leaves at least the day before
they are needed.

1 Dust the work surface with a little powdered sugar, then knead the caramel gum paste until it is soft and pliable. Roll out the kneaded gum paste quite thinly and stamp out a leaf using the 1in. veined leaf plunger cutter. While the gum paste is still soft, mold the leaf into a slightly curved shape. Stamping and molding one leaf at a time, repeat with the remaining gum paste to make 12 leaves in total. Place the leaves on the indented foam pad—this will help the leaves to keep their curved shape as they dry. Allow the leaves to dry overnight, uncovered, in a cool, dry place.

2 The next day, put the powdered sugar, ground almonds, butter and heaped 1⅓ cups of the flour in a food processor and pulse about 15 seconds until the mixture resembles coarse breadcrumbs. Add 1 of the egg yolks and pulse until the mixture just comes together to form a dough. If the dough is too dry, gradually add 1–2 tablespoons of cold water, one tablespoon at a time. Shape the dough into a ball, handling it as little as possible. Seal in plastic wrap and chill in the refrigerator at least 30 minutes.

3 Preheat the oven to 350°F and lightly grease the muffin pan with butter. Unwrap the dough and turn it out onto a sheet of parchment paper lightly dusted with powdered sugar, then lay another sheet of parchment paper on top. Roll out the dough between the two sheets until it is about ¼in. thick, using marzipan spacers if you like. Cut out 12 pastry circles with the 3½in. fluted cookie cutter, then gently press them into the prepared muffin cups.

4 Cut out 12 squares of parchment paper, each large enough to cover a pastry shell. Prick each pastry shell a few times with a fork, then line with a square of parchment paper and fill with baking beans. Blind bake the pastry shells 15 minutes or until golden brown. Remove from the oven and leave in the pan to cool a little, then gently ease the pastry shells out of the muffin pan and transfer to a wire rack. Leave to cool completely.

5 To make the crème pâtissière, put the remaining egg yolks, 2 tablespoons of the superfine sugar and the vanilla extract in a large mixing bowl and whisk until pale. Sift in the remaining flour and whisk until combined. Put the milk and the remaining superfine sugar in a saucepan over medium-low heat and bring just to a boil. Remove from the heat and leave to cool 1 minute. Gradually pour the hot milk into the egg mixture, whisking continuously. Return the mixture to the saucepan and return to a boil over medium-low heat, stirring constantly, 5 minutes or until thick and glossy. Pour the crème pâtissière into a clean bowl and cover with plastic wrap, making sure the plastic wrap touches the surface of the crème pâtissière to stop a skin from forming. Leave to cool completely. Meanwhile, put a little gold edible lustre dust in a small bowl. Add water, a few drops at a time, and mix until a thick paint forms. Paint the leaves with the lustre paint and leave to dry completely. When the gum-paste leaves have dried and the crème pâtissière has cooled, spoon the crème pâtissière into the pastry bag, then snip off the end if necessary. Pipe a layer of crème pâtissière in each pastry case, add a layer of fruit and decorate with gold leaves and a dusting of powdered sugar.

Raspberry Dust Macarons

MAKES 30 MACARONS
3 large egg whites
¼ cup superfine sugar
pink food coloring paste
1¼ cups powdered sugar
1 cup ground almonds
2 tbsp. freeze-dried raspberry fruit powder
scant ½ cup seedless raspberry jam

YOU WILL NEED
electric mixer
toothpicks
4 piping guide templates (see page 170)
2 baking sheets
parchment paper
pastry bag with a ½in. plain tip attached
small angled metal spatula

1 Put the egg whites in a mixing bowl and beat with the electric mixer 2 minutes, or until they just start to form soft peaks—if your egg whites are very fresh you may have to beat a little longer. With the mixer running, gradually add the sugar and continue to beat until the mixture is thick and glossy but not too stiff. Add a small amount of pink food coloring paste to the mixture, using the end of a toothpick, and gently whisk until combined. Repeat until the desired color is achieved, bearing in mind that the color of the mixture will fade slightly when baked.

2 Sift the powdered sugar and ground almonds into a separate mixing bowl. Add one-third of the pink meringue mixture and gently fold it into the powdered sugar and ground almonds until incorporated. Add the remaining pink meringue mixture and fold until completely incorporated.

3 Using a spatula, press and spread the mixture up the side of the bowl. Repeat this about ten times, letting the mixture drop back down into the bowl, until the macaron mixture is smooth and has a slow-dropping consistency—this process helps to give the macarons their shine once baked.

4 Set 2 piping guides over each baking sheet, then place a sheet of parchment paper over the top of each guide. Spoon the macaron mixture into the pastry bag. Using the piping guide as a template, pipe out 60 large dots of macaron mixture onto the baking sheets—take care not to pipe outside the circle outlines on the guides because the mixture will spread a little once piped. (For hints on piping, see pages 157–9.) Carefully slide the piping guides off the baking sheets, leaving the parchment paper in place.

5 Sharply tap the baking sheets on the work surface a few times to remove any air bubbles from the macarons—this also helps to smooth the mixture and create a frilly "foot." Lightly sprinkle the dried raspberry powder over the top of 30 of the macarons with a teaspoon. Leave the macarons, uncovered, in a cool, dry place until a very light crust forms over the top of each one and they are dry to the touch—this should take about 15 to 45 minutes depending on room temperature and humidity. Meanwhile, preheat the oven to 275°F.

6 Bake the macarons 13 to 15 minutes, or until the macarons can be lifted cleanly off the parchment paper with the angled metal spatula. Remove from the oven and, without removing the macarons, slide the sheets of parchment paper onto wire racks and leave to cool completely.

7 When the macarons have cooled, carefully remove them from the parchment paper with the angled metal spatula. Spoon 1 teaspoon of jam onto the flat sides of the plain macarons, taking care to spoon the jam into the center to prevent it from spreading out over the side when you sandwich the macarons together. Sandwich together the jam-covered halves with the raspberry-dusted halves to make 30 filled macarons in total.

Chocolate-Dipped Florentines

MAKES 8 FLORENTINES
1½ tbsp. salted butter
¼ cup + 1½ tbsp. golden superfine sugar
3 tbsp. heavy cream
1 heaped tbsp. all-purpose flour
scant 1 cup flaked almonds
¼ cup stem ginger in syrup, drained and finely diced
finely grated zest of 1 orange
5½oz. dark or milk chocolate, or half of each

YOU WILL NEED
8 x 8in. baking pan lined with parchment paper (for hints on lining baking pans, see page 149)
sharp knife
baking sheet lined with parchment paper

1 Preheat the oven to 350°F. Put the butter, sugar and cream in a saucepan over medium heat. Stir continuously until the butter has melted and the sugar has dissolved. Stir in the flour, then add the almonds, stem ginger and orange zest and cook, stirring continuously, until thoroughly combined. Remove the pan from the heat.

2 Spoon the mixture into the prepared baking pan, then level with a metal spoon. Bake 13 minutes, or until golden brown. Remove from the oven and leave to cool in the pan 5 minutes. Without removing the parchment paper, transfer the florentine from the pan to a cutting board. While it is still warm, cut the florentine into 8 fingers with the sharp knife. Transfer the fingers to a wire rack and leave to cool completely.

3 Put the chocolate in a heatproof bowl and rest it over a saucepan of gently simmering water, making sure the bottom of the bowl does not touch the water. Heat, stirring occasionally, until melted. Alternatively, put the chocolate in a bowl and microwave, uncovered, on medium 2 minutes until melted, stirring every 30 seconds to ensure the chocolate does not burn.

4 Dip the end of each florentine finger into the melted chocolate, then transfer to the prepared baking sheet. Leave the florentines at least 10 to 15 minutes, uncovered, in a cool, dry place to allow the chocolate to set.

Marble Swirl Mini Meringues

MAKES 30 MERINGUES
2 large egg whites
½ cup superfine sugar
2 tsp. rosewater
pink food coloring paste

YOU WILL NEED
2 piping guide templates
  (see page 170)
2 baking sheets
parchment paper
electric mixer
baking pan
pastry bag with a ½in. plain tip
  attached
small angled metal spatula

1 Preheat the oven to 225°F. Place a piping guide onto each baking sheet, then set a sheet of parchment paper on top of each guide. Put the egg whites in a mixing bowl and beat with the electric mixer until they start to form soft peaks. With the mixer running, gradually add the sugar and continue to beat until the mixture is thick and glossy. Gently stir in the rosewater.

2 Pour the meringue mixture into the baking pan, spreading it out over the bottom of the pan. Using a fork, dot the meringue mixture with a little pink food coloring paste, then drag the fork through the mixture to create a marbled pattern **(a)**, bearing in mind that the color of the mixture will fade slightly when baked.

3 Gently spoon the meringue mixture into the pastry bag, taking care to keep the marbled pattern intact **(b)**—this will maximize the marbled effect when piping. Using the piping guide as a template, pipe out 30 meringue swirls onto the baking sheets, starting from the edge of the circles and swirling toward the center **(c)**. (For hints on piping, see pages 157–9.) Carefully slide the piping guides off the baking sheets, leaving the parchment paper in place.

4 Bake 45 to 60 minutes, or until the meringues can be lifted cleanly off the parchment paper with the angled metal spatula. If the meringues stick to the parchment, bake a further 10 to 15 minutes before testing again. When the meringues are ready, turn off the oven and open the door slightly. Leave the meringues in the cooling oven 20 minutes, then remove and carefully lift each one off the parchment paper with the angled metal spatula. Leave to cool completely.

(a)

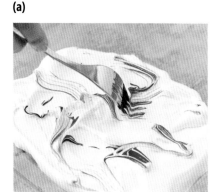

(b)

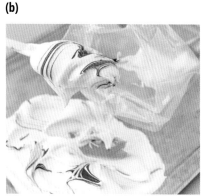

(c)

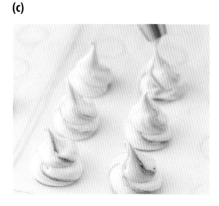

CHAPTER TWO

Certain occasions provide the perfect excuse to treat our loved ones. Whether it's with a Chocolate Heart Cake Pop on Valentine's Day to say "I love you," a batch of Wedding Favor Blossom Cookies to say "Thank you for sharing our special day," or a cake topped with handmade truffles to celebrate that milestone anniversary, you'll create wonderful memories.

DECORATE

FOR

LOVE

Kissing Birds Cookies

MAKES 30 COOKIES
(15 PAIRS)
powdered sugar, for dusting
7oz. bright pink-colored gum
  paste (see pages 160–1)
¾ cup white stiff-peak Royal
  Icing (see page 46)
30 cookies made using
  1 recipe quantity Cookie
  Dough of your choice (see
  pages 26–7) cut out with
  a bird cookie cutter
edible glue or 2 tbsp. apricot
  jam, warmed

YOU WILL NEED
small rolling pin
small culinary stencil
small angled metal spatula
bird cookie cutter
small paintbrush
small pastry bag with
  a no. 2 plain tip

HINT
To make the birds in "kissing"
pairs, cut out half the birds facing
right and half facing left. To
achieve a mirrored stencil design
on the facing birds, simply turn
the stencil over before you place
it on top of the gum paste.

1 Dust the work surface with a little powdered sugar, then take about ¾oz. of the gum paste and knead until it is soft and pliable. Keep the remaining gum paste in an airtight container until needed so it does not dry out and crack. Roll out the kneaded gum paste quite thinly.

2 Place your stencil in the center of the gum paste and lightly hold it in place with one hand—if the stencil moves, the design may smudge. Using the angled metal spatula, spread a little royal icing over the stencil **(a)**. Remove any excess royal icing with the metal spatula, then carefully peel back the stencil.

3 Immediately position the bird cookie cutter over the stenciled design **(b)**. When you're happy with the effect, cut out a bird from the gum paste. Roll the trimmings into a ball and add to the remaining gum paste. Brush the surface of one of the cookies with edible glue. Clean the angled metal spatula, then place the gum paste bird onto the prepared cookie, taking care not to stretch the gum paste. Working on one cookie at a time and dusting the work surface with powdered sugar as necessary, repeat with the remaining gum paste, royal icing, cookies and edible glue to make 30 decorated cookies in total. Remember to wash and dry the stencil thoroughly before decorating each cookie.

4 To finish, spoon the remaining royal icing into the pastry bag and pipe a closed eye onto the face of each bird (see picture). (For hints on piping, see pages 157–9.) Leave the cookies at least 1 hour, uncovered, in a cool, dry place to allow the decoration to set.

(a)

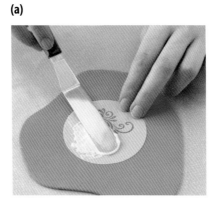

(b)

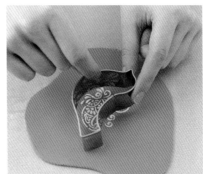

Glitter Filigree Cookies

MAKES 12 COOKIES
12 cookies made using ½ recipe quantity Cookie Dough of your choice (see pages 26–7), cut out with the heart template (see page 162) or with a heart cookie cutter, just baked
¼ cup purple-colored soft-peak Royal Icing (see page 46)
purple, white and gold edible glitters
¼ cup white soft-peak Royal Icing (see page 46)
¼ cup caramel-colored soft-peak Royal Icing (see page 46)

YOU WILL NEED
¼in. round circle cutter (optional)
parchment paper
3 pastry bags, each with a no. 2 plain tip attached
small paintbrush
3 x ¼in. wide ribbon in purple, ivory and gold, each 39in. long and each cut into 4 equal pieces (optional)
toothpick, if needed

HINT
Use different food coloring pastes, edible glitters and ribbons to create your own color scheme.

1 As soon as the cookies come out of the oven, and while they are still hot, carefully stamp out a small hole at the top of each one with the ¼in. circle cutter or with the end of a drinking straw. Then transfer to a wire rack and leave to cool completely.

2 When the cookies have cooled, set three sheets of parchment paper on the work surface and place 4 cookies on each one. Spoon the purple soft-peak royal icing into one of the pastry bags. Decorating one cookie at a time and using the picture as a guide, pipe a heart outline around the cookie, then pipe the filigree design using curvy lines and dots **(a)**. Dip the end of a teaspoon into the purple edible glitter, then, holding the spoon in one hand, gently tap the handle with the other to lightly dust the icing with glitter **(b)**. Working in color batches, repeat step 2 continuing to ice and glitter one cookie at a time to make 12 decorated cookies in total, then leave at least 1 hour, uncovered, in a cool, dry place to allow the icing to set.

3 When the icing has completely set, gently remove any excess glitter from the cookies with a paintbrush and tip any excess glitter on the sheets of parchment paper back into their pots. Take a piece of purple ribbon and carefully thread it through the hole of a cookie with purple icing, using the toothpick to help push the ribbon through the hole if necessary, then finish with a bow, if you like. Repeat with the remaining cookies and ribbons to make 12 finished cookies.

(a)

(b)

Royal Icing

MAKES ABOUT 1LB. 5OZ.
2 tbsp. pasteurized dried egg
    white powder or 2 large
    egg whites
4 cups powdered sugar
squeeze of lemon juice
food coloring pastes (optional)

YOU WILL NEED
electric mixer
toothpick (optional)

HINT
Royal icing can be stored up to
7 days in an airtight container in
the refrigerator. The icing may split
during storage, so make sure you
whisk it thoroughly before use.

Depending on its purpose, royal icing is made up to one of three consistencies: stiff-peak, soft-peak and flood-consistency. It can be colored any shade you want. Simply add a small amount of food coloring paste to the icing using the end of a toothpick, and mix until combined. Repeat until the desired color is achieved. (For extra hints on consistency, and for hints on piping intricate details, see page 159.)

Stiff-Peak Royal Icing

Stiff-peak royal icing is traditionally used to cover Christmas and celebration cakes. It is often used to attach large, heavy decorations to cakes or to secure decorations that need to be held in a vertical position. It can also be used to attach cakes to cake boards and to secure tiers of a cake during stacking. To make stiff-peak royal icing, put ⅓ cup boiling water in a small bowl and leave to cool completely. When the water has cooled, add the dried egg-white powder, if using, to the bowl and mix well. Cover with plastic wrap and chill in the refrigerator at least a few hours or overnight. Sift the powdered sugar into a mixing bowl. Add the reconstituted dried egg whites (or fresh egg whites if using) and lemon juice and beat with the electric mixer until just combined, then beat 5 minutes until the mixture forms stiff peaks. Immediately transfer to an airtight container.

Soft-Peak Royal Icing

Soft-peak royal icing is used to pipe outlines onto cookies before they are flooded (see below). It can also be used to pipe decorative lines and dots onto cakes and cookies, and to attach smaller, lighter decorations to cakes. To make soft-peak royal icing, make a batch of stiff-peak royal icing as above, then stir in cold water, a few drops at a time, until the icing slackens a little and forms soft peaks. Immediately transfer to an airtight container.

Flood-Consistency Royal Icing

Flood-consistency royal icing is used to fill or "flood" the middle of cookies outlined with soft-peak royal icing. To make flood-consistency royal icing, make a batch of stiff-peak royal icing as above, then stir in cold water, a few drops at a time, until the icing slackens completely and has a smooth pouring consistency similar to heavy cream. Immediately transfer to an airtight container.

Use this royal icing recipe for the following recipes throughout this book:

 **Gingerbread Family**
page 25

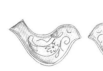 **Kissing Birds Cookies**
page 42

 Glitter Filigree Cookies
page 45

 Corset Cookies
page 50

 Chocolate Box Cake with Truffles
page 52

 **Wedding Favor Blossom Cookies**
page 58

 **Christmas Wreath Tree Decorations**
page 72

 **Gingerbread House**
page 78

 **Thanksgiving Cookies**
page 83

 **White Blossom Christening Cake**
page 84

 Festive Ball Cakes
page 92

 **Easter Hen Cookies**
page 99

 **Birthday Butterfly Mini Domes**
page 104

 **Santa's Sleigh Cake**
page 107

 **Ivory Corsage Wedding Cake**
page 114

 Butterfly Fancies
page 116

 Magnificent Mini Cakes
page 121

 **Teapot Cake**
page 122

 **Hydrangea Cake**
page 130

 **Flower Cake Pops**
page 132

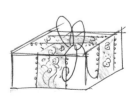 **Gift-Wrapped Cake**
page 135

Valentine Cigarillo Cake

MAKES 1 CAKE
2 x 6in. round Marble Cakes
   (see pages 76–7)
1 recipe quantity Vanilla
   Buttercream (see page 16)
70 x 4in. white chocolate
   cigarillos
1 cup white chocolate chips
2 cups strawberries at room
   temperature

YOU WILL NEED
6in. round cake board
39in. pale pink chiffon ribbon,
   1½in. wide (optional)
baking sheet lined with
   parchment paper

HINTS
Chocolate cigarillos are widely
available online. For larger round
cakes you will need:
80 cigarillos for 7in.
90 cigarillos for 8in.
100 cigarillos for 9in.
110 cigarillos for 10in.

Heating and cooling chocolate
without controlling the
temperature (tempering) causes
blemishes to appear on the
surface. The chocolate will also
crumble rather than snap. Adding
unmelted chocolate to melted
chocolate (see step 3) is a simple
and easy way to temper chocolate.

1 Following the instructions on page 150 and using the cake board as a base, layer the cakes, then fill with buttercream to make one tall cake. Following the instructions on page 152, cover the cake with the remaining buttercream. The cake should be no taller than 3in. If it is too high the cigarillos will not rise above the cake and the chocolate-dipped strawberries will fall off the top. Chill the cake in the refrigerator 2 hours.

2 When the buttercream has set, gently press the cigarillos vertically into the side of the cake, making sure they are as straight as possible and squarely lined up at the base **(a)**—the buttercream will hold them in position. Hold the cigarillos as lightly as possible to prevent them from melting. Tie the ribbon around the cake and finish with a bow, if you like.

3 Put half of the white chocolate chips in a heatproof bowl and rest it over a saucepan of gently simmering water, making sure the bottom of the bowl does not touch the water. Heat, stirring occasionally, until melted. Alternatively, put the chocolate chips in a bowl and microwave, uncovered, on medium 2 minutes until melted, stirring every 30 seconds to ensure the chocolate does not burn. Remove the pan from the heat and add the remaining chocolate chips, stirring until the chips have melted and the mixture has thickened slightly.

4 Holding them by the stalks, dip the tip of each strawberry into the melted chocolate. Lift the strawberries out of the coating, allowing any excess chocolate to fall back into the bowl, then transfer them to the prepared baking sheet. Leave the coated strawberries at least 10 to 15 minutes, uncovered, at room temperature to allow the chocolate to set. Do not chill the strawberries in the refrigerator.

5 When the chocolate has set, pile the chocolate-dipped strawberries on top of the cake and eat within 1 day.

(a)

Corset Cookies

MAKES 12 COOKIES
1 cup pale pink-colored soft-
  peak Royal Icing (see page 46)
12 cookies made using ½ recipe
  quantity Cookie Dough of your
  choice (see pages 26–7), cut
  out with the corset template
  (see page 162)
¼ cup white soft-peak Royal
  Icing (see page 46)

YOU WILL NEED
pastry bag with a no. 2 plain
  tip attached
plastic squeeze bottle
pastry bag with a no. 1.5
  plain tip attached

HINT
For a more dramatic look, outline
and flood the cookie with red
icing and use black icing for the
corset detail.

1 Spoon the pale pink soft-peak royal icing into the pastry bag with the no. 2 plain tip attached to it. Pipe a corset outline onto each cookie **(a)**. (For hints on piping, see pages 157–9.) Leave the cookies at least 10 to 15 minutes, uncovered, in a cool, dry place to allow the icing to set.

2 Spoon the remaining pale pink soft-peak royal icing into a bowl and add enough water to slacken it to flood consistency (see page 46). Pour the flood icing into the plastic squeeze bottle and flood the center of each cookie **(b)**. Leave the cookies at least 1 hour, uncovered, in a cool, dry place to allow the icing to set.

3 When the icing has set, spoon the white soft-peak royal icing into the pastry bag with the no. 1.5 plain tip attached to it. Decorating one cookie at a time and using the picture as a guide, pipe the white lace detail onto each cookie **(c)**. Leave the cookies overnight, uncovered, in a cool, dry place to allow the icing to set completely.

(a)

(b)

(c)

Chocolate Box Cake with Truffles

MAKES 25 TRUFFLES
14oz. baking chocolate,
 70% cocoa solids, broken
 into small pieces
scant 1 cup heavy cream
scant ½ cup powdered sugar
unsweetened cocoa powder,
 for dusting (optional)

YOU WILL NEED
1⅓in. spring-action release
 ice-cream scoop (optional)
baking sheet lined with
 parchment paper
chocolate dipping fork (optional)

HINT
If the mixture splits, warm up a
little more cream, add it to the
mixture and stir until smooth.

TRUFFLES

1 Put 9oz. of the chocolate in a heatproof bowl. Pour the cream into a small saucepan and bring just to a boil on medium-low heat. Pour the cream over the chocolate in the bowl **(a)** and leave to stand 5 minutes until the chocolate has melted **(b)**. Make sure to stir occasionally, but take care not to overmix or the mixture will split. Add the powdered sugar and stir until smooth. Leave to cool completely, then chill in the refrigerator 1 to 2 hours until firm.

2 When the mixture is firm, scoop out a walnut-sized piece, using the ice cream scoop or tablespoon **(c)**, then gently roll it into a ball. Transfer the truffle to the prepared baking sheet and repeat with the remaining mixture to make 25 to 30 truffles. Chill in the refrigerator until needed.

3 Put the remaining chocolate in a heatproof bowl and rest it over a saucepan of gently simmering water, making sure the bottom of the bowl does not touch the water. Heat, stirring occasionally, until melted. Alternatively, put the chocolate in a bowl and microwave, uncovered, on medium 2 minutes until melted, stirring every 30 seconds to ensure the chocolate does not burn.

(a)   **(b)**   **(c)**

(d)   **(e)**   **(f)**

4 Drop one of the truffles into the melted chocolate. Using the chocolate dipping fork or a dinner fork, gently twist the truffle through the chocolate until it is completely coated **(d)**. Lift the truffle out of the coating, allowing any excess chocolate to fall back into the bowl **(e)**. Return the chocolate-coated truffle to the prepared baking sheet, then repeat with the remaining truffles and melted chocolate until all the truffles are coated. Return the baking sheet to the refrigerator and leave to chill until the coating has set. When set, remove the truffles from the refrigerator and lightly dust with unsweetened cocoa powder, if you like **(f)**. Transfer to an airtight container and chill in the refrigerator until needed.

MAKES 1 FLOWER
powdered sugar, for dusting
1½oz. pale yellow-colored gum paste (see pages 160–1)
1½oz. white gum paste (see pages 160–1)
edible glue or cooled, boiled water

YOU WILL NEED
small rolling pin
sharp knife
small, medium and large flower templates (see page 167) or 1⅓in., 1¾in. and 2½in. flower cutters
modeling pad or a clean, dry folded tea towel
veiner tool
indented foam pad or a piece of crinkled aluminum foil
small paintbrush

CHOCOLATE BOX

For the Flower

1 Dust the work surface with a little powdered sugar, then knead the gum pastes until they are soft and pliable. Roll out the pale yellow gum paste quite thinly and cut out a small flower and a large flower using the small and large flower templates. Roll out half of the white gum paste quite thinly and cut out a medium flower using the medium template. Roll a little of the white gum paste trimmings into a pea-sized ball and set it aside to firm up a little.

2 Place the flowers on the modeling pad, then roll the veiner tool over each petal to create a textured effect **(g)**. Place the largest flower on the indented foam pad. Brush a little edible glue in the center of the largest flower, then lay the medium flower over the top. Repeat using a little more edible glue to attach the small flower to the center of the medium flower **(h)**. Attach the pea-sized ball of white gum paste to the center of the flower with a little edible glue **(i)**. Leave the flower to dry overnight, uncovered, in a cool, dry place.

(g)

(h)

(i)

**MAKES 2 LEAVES,
1 GIFT TAG AND THE
CHOCOLATE BOX**
powdered sugar, for dusting
1oz. green-colored gum paste
   (see pages 160–1)
15oz. white gum paste (see
   pages 160–1)
8in. Rich Chocolate Heart Cake
   (see pages 56–7)
1 recipe quantity Vanilla
   Buttercream (see page 16)
1lb. 9oz. pale yellow-colored
   gum paste (see pages 160–1)
¼ cup white soft-peak Royal
   Icing (see page 46)

YOU WILL NEED
rolling pin
sharp knife
leaf template (see page 167)
modeling pad or a clean, dry
   folded tea towel
veiner tool
ruler
¼in. circle cutter or the end
   of a drinking straw
design wheeler tool with stitch
   head
8in. heart-shaped cake board
¼in. marzipan spacers
   (optional)
8in. heart-shaped cake pan
icing smoother
8in. yellow ribbon, ½in. wide
pastry bag with a no. 2 plain
   tip attached

For the Leaves, Gift Tag and Chocolate Box

1 Dust the work surface with a little powdered sugar, then knead the green gum paste and 1¾oz. of the white gum paste until they are soft and pliable. To make the leaves, roll out the green gum paste quite thinly and cut out 2 leaves using the leaf template. Place the leaves on the modeling pad, then roll the veiner tool over the leaves to create a textured effect. Pinch the gum paste together at the base of the leaves to form an inward curve **(j)**.

2 To make the gift tag, roll out 1¾oz. of the white gum paste quite thinly and cut out a 3¼ x 2in. rectangle. Cut one end to a point and stamp out a small hole with the ¼in. circle cutter. Use the design wheeler tool to indent a "stitched" line around the edge of the tag **(k)**. Leave the leaves and gift tag to dry overnight, uncovered, in a cool, dry place.

3 When the decorations have dried, follow the instructions on page 150 and layer the cake, then fill with buttercream. Following the instructions on page 152 and using the cake board as a firm base, cover the cake with the remaining buttercream. Chill in the refrigerator 2 hours until set. When the buttercream has set, dust the work surface with a little powdered sugar, then knead the remaining white gum paste, and the pale yellow gum paste until they are soft and pliable. Roll out the white gum paste until it is ¼in. thick, using marzipan spacers if you like. Using the cake pan as a template, cut out a heart shape from the gum paste. Lay the heart on top of the cake, smoothing it down with your hands and then with the icing smoother.

4 To make the sides of the box, roll out the pale yellow gum paste until it is ¼in. thick, using marzipan spacers if you like, and cut out a 28 x 2¾in. rectangle. Attach it to the side of the cake **(l)**, smoothing it down with your hands and then with the icing smoother and trimming as necessary. The rectangle should cover the sides and be tall enough to create a shallow "box" on top of the cake. Attach the ribbon to the gift tag. Spoon the royal icing into the pastry bag and pipe a message onto the gift tag if you like, such as "with love," then pipe a polka-dot design around the sides of the cake. (For hints on piping, see pages 157–9). Arrange the truffles in the "box" and top with the decorations, securing them with the remaining royal icing. Allow the icing to set before serving.

(j)

(k)

(l)

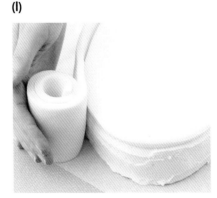

Rich Chocolate Cake

salted butter
baking chocolate, 70% cocoa
 solids
coffee extract
egg(s)
milk
self-rising flour
all-purpose flour
baking soda
unsweetened cocoa powder
superfine sugar

YOU WILL NEED
**cake pan(s) lined with
 parchment paper (for hints on
 lining cake pans, see page 149)**

HINT
If the cake is going to be split into
layers, wrap it in parchment paper
and aluminum foil, then leave it to
rest overnight to firm up a little.
This will make it easier to cut.
(For hints on layering, filling and
covering cakes, see pages 150
and 152–3.)

**The table opposite shows you the quantity of ingredients and baking times required
for different cake sizes and styles. It also offers advice on serving portions. Simply
select your size and style and follow the method below.**

1 Preheat the oven to 315°F. Melt the butter and chocolate in a saucepan over medium-low heat.
Add the coffee extract to the pan and stir until combined, then pour the mixture into a large mixing
bowl.

2 In a large measuring jug, lightly beat together the egg(s) and milk. Pour the egg mixture into the
chocolate mixture, stirring to combine. In another bowl, sift together the flours, baking soda and
unsweetened cocoa powder. Gradually add small quantities of the flour mixture to the chocolate
mixture, making sure it is well incorporated before adding more. Add the sugar and stir until
combined—the batter should be fairly runny by this stage.

3 Spoon the batter into the prepared cake pan(s), leveling the surface with the back of a spoon.
Bake for the recommended time or until a skewer inserted into the center comes out clean. Oven
temperatures can vary, so check on the cake(s) about 5 minutes before the end of the recommended
baking time.

4 Remove the cake(s) from the oven and leave to cool 5 minutes, then remove from the pan,
transfer to a wire rack and leave to cool completely.

Use this rich chocolate sponge recipe for the following recipes throughout this book:

Chocolate Fan Cake
page 30

**Chocolate Box Cake
with Truffles**
page 52

Festive Ball Cakes
page 92

Christmas Pudding Cake
page 97

**Ivory Corsage
Wedding Cake**
page 114

	4in. round or square cake 6 cupcakes	5in. round or square cake	6in. round or square cake 4 x 3¼in. mini ball cake halves 24 mini cupcakes	7in. round or square cake	8in. round, square or heart cake 12 cupcakes	9in. round or square cake 2 x 6in ball cake halves
salted butter	3½ tbsp.	⅓ cup (⅔ stick)	scant ½ cup (¾ stick)	⅔ cup (1⅓ sticks)	1 cup (2 sticks)	1⅓ cups (2⅔ sticks)
baking chocolate, 70% cocoa solids	1oz.	1¼oz.	1¾oz.	2½oz.	3½oz.	5½oz.
coffee extract	1 tsp.	1 tsp.	2 tsp.	1 tbsp.	1 tbsp. plus 1 tsp.	2 tbsp.
eggs	1 medium	1 large	2 medium	2 large	3 large	5 medium
milk	1½ tbsp.	2½ tbsp.	3½ tbsp.	⅓ cup	scant ½ cup	scant ⅔ cup
self-rising flour	scant ¼ cup	heaped ¼ cup	scant ½ cup	scant ⅔ cup	heaped ¾ cup	scant 1¼ cups
all-purpose flour	scant ¼ cup	heaped ¼ cup	scant ½ cup	scant ⅔ cup	heaped ¾ cup	scant 1¼ cups
baking soda	¼ tsp.	¼ tsp.	¼ tsp.	½ tsp.	½ tsp.	¾ tsp.
unsweetened cocoa powder	2 tsp.	1 tbsp.	scant ¼ cup	¼ cup	⅓ cup	½ cup
superfine sugar	scant ⅓ cup	scant ½ cup	heaped ⅔ cup	scant 1 cup	scant 1⅓ cups	scant 2 cups
baking time	20 minutes for large cakes	25 minutes	30 minutes for large cakes	40 minutes	50 minutes for large cakes	1 hour 10 minutes for large cakes
	15 minutes for cupcakes		15 minutes for mini ball cake halves		15 minutes for cupcakes	45 minutes for ball cake halves
			8 minutes for mini cupcakes			
serves	large cakes: 10	12	large cakes: 15–20	20–30	large cakes: 30–40	large cakes: 40–50
	cupcakes: 6		mini ball cake halves: 4		cupcakes: 12	ball cake halves: 12–16
			mini cupcakes: 24			

Wedding Favor Blossom Cookies

MAKES 30 COOKIES
¾ cup pale blue-colored soft-peak Royal Icing (see page 46)
30 cookies made using 1 recipe quantity Cookie Dough of your choice (see pages 26–7), cut out with the small, medium and large blossom templates (see page 165) to make 10 cookies of each size
⅓ cup white sugar pearls
¾ cup ivory-colored soft-peak Royal Icing (see page 46)

YOU WILL NEED
2 pastry bags, each with a no. 2 plain tip attached
2 plastic squeeze bottles

HINT
For perfect presentation, transfer the finished cookies to cellophane gift bags and tie each one with a piece of ribbon.

1 Spoon a heaped ¼ cup of the pale blue soft-peak royal icing into one of the pastry bags. Pipe a blossom outline around half of the cookies, then leave at least 10 to 15 minutes, uncovered, in a cool, dry place to allow the icing to set. Roll up the pastry bag and store in an airtight container until needed. (For hints on piping, see pages 157–9.)

2 Spoon the remaining pale blue soft-peak royal icing into a bowl and add enough water to slacken it to flood consistency (see page 46). Pour the flood icing into one of the plastic squeeze bottles and flood the center of one of the cookies. Before the icing sets, drop a sugar pearl into the center of the blossom shape. Carefully place another 6 sugar pearls around the central pearl to form a blossom shape. Flooding one cookie at a time, repeat with the remaining pale blue flood icing, outlined cookies and sugar pearls to make 15 iced cookies. Leave the cookies at least 1 hour, uncovered, in a cool, dry place to allow the icing to set. Meanwhile, repeat steps 1 and 2 with the ivory soft-peak royal icing and the remaining cookies and sugar pearls to make 30 decorated cookies in total.

3 When the icing has set, pipe another blossom outline around the edge of each cookie with the remaining pale blue and ivory soft-peak royal icings. Leave the cookies overnight, uncovered, in a cool, dry place to allow the icing to completely set.

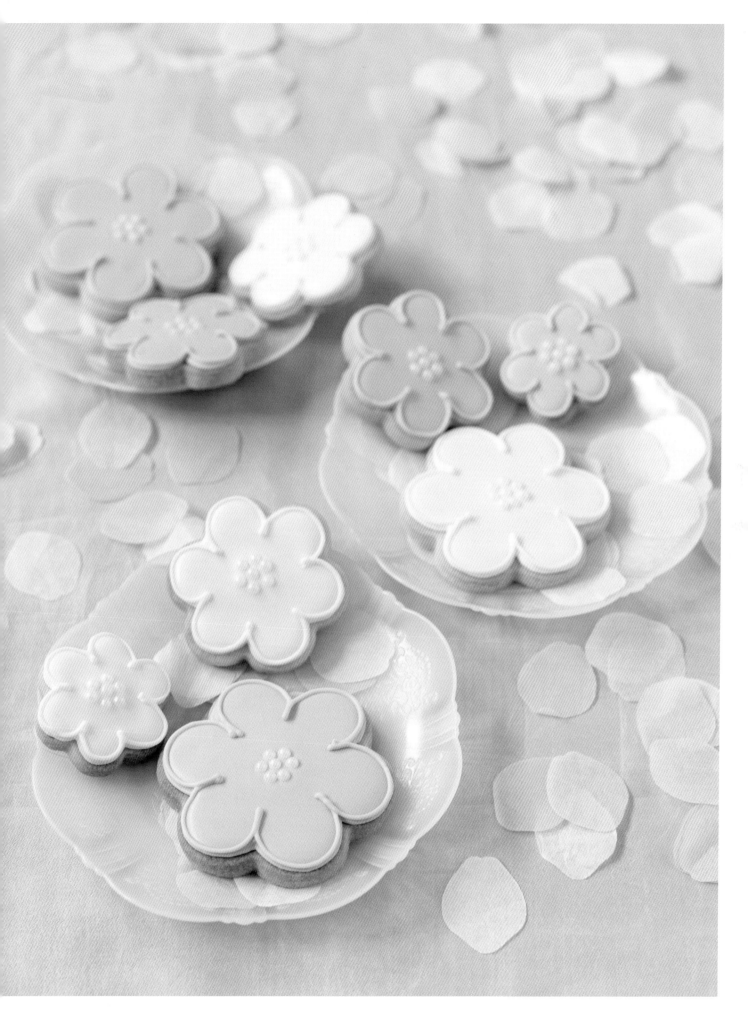

Pom Pom Wedding Cake

MAKES 1 CAKE
2 x 9in. round Vanilla Sponge
    Cakes (see pages 62–3)
2 x 6in. round Basic Sponge
    Cakes (see pages 62–3)
2 recipe quantities Vanilla
    Buttercream (see page 16)
powdered sugar, for dusting
3lb. 8oz. ivory-colored gum
    paste (see pages 160–1)
edible glue or cooled, boiled
    water
7oz. pale pink-colored gum
    paste (pages 160–1)

YOU WILL NEED
9in. round cake board
6in. round cake board
plastic dowel rods
10in. piece ivory satin ribbon,
    1in. wide
small paintbrush
6½in. piece ivory satin ribbon
    1in. wide
small rolling pin
sharp knife
ruler
⅝in. circle cutter
4 sheets of ivory tissue paper
scissors
small piece of florist's wire

1 Following the instructions on page 150 and using the cake boards as firm bases, layer the cakes, then fill with buttercream to make one tall 9in. cake and one tall 6in. cake. Following the instructions on page 152, cover the cakes with the remaining buttercream. Chill in the refrigerator at least 2 hours. When the buttercream has set, dust the work surface with a little powdered sugar, then knead 2lb. 4oz. of the ivory gum paste until it is soft and pliable. Following the instructions on page 153, cover the 9in. cake with the kneaded gum paste. Repeat with the remaining gum paste to cover the 6in. cake. Leave the cakes overnight, uncovered, in a cool, dry place to allow the gum paste to dry. When the gum paste has dried, follow the instructions on page 156 and stack the 6in. cake on top of 9in. cake with plastic dowel rods. Wrap the 10in. ribbon around the base of the bottom tier, securing the join at the back with a little edible glue and trimming if necessary, then attach the 6½in. ribbon to the base of the top tier.

2 Dust the work surface with powdered sugar, then knead half of the pale pink gum paste and roll out quite thinly. For the stripes, cut 12 strips of rolled gum paste, each about 4 x ⅝in. using the sharp knife. Position the strips around the top tier of the cake, making sure they are evenly spaced, as straight as possible and squarely lined up with the ribbon, then secure with edible glue. For the dots, knead the remaining pale pink gum paste and roll out quite thinly. Stamp out 36 circles with the ⅝in. circle cutter. Brush the back of each circle with a little edible glue, then attach them to the bottom tier in three rows (see picture).

3 To make the pom pom, lay out the sheets of tissue paper, one on top of the other, and cut out a rectangle about 10 x 6in. Crease the paper along the short edge into concertina folds, each about 1¼in. deep. Fold and crease the concertinaed paper in half, then wrap the florist's wire over this central crease **(a)**, twisting to secure and trimming the wire if necessary. Using scissors, round off the ends of the paper for a neat finish **(b)**. Separate the layers by gently pulling them apart and upward to form a dome shape **(c)**, then place the finished pom pom on top of the cake.

(a)

(b)

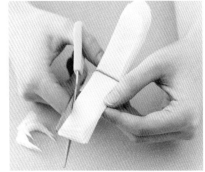

(c)

Basic Sponge Cake

salted butter
superfine sugar
egg(s)
self-rising flour
vanilla extract (optional)
unsweetened cocoa powder
  (optional)
lemon or orange zest (optional)
coffee extract (optional)

YOU WILL NEED
electric mixer
cake pan(s) lined with
  parchment paper (for hints on
  lining cake pans, see page 149)

HINT
If the cake is going to be split
into layers, wrap it in parchment
paper and foil, then leave it to rest
overnight to firm up a little. This
will make it easier to cut (for hints
on layering, filling and covering
cakes, see pages 150–153).

The table opposite shows you the quantity of ingredients and baking times required for different cake sizes and styles. It also offers advice on serving portions. Simply select your size and style and follow the method below.

1 Preheat the oven to 350°F and allow the butter to soften slightly. Put the sugar and the softened butter in a mixing bowl and beat with the electric mixer about 3 minutes until light and fluffy. Lightly beat the egg(s), then gradually add to the mixture. If the mixture starts to curdle, add a little of the flour. Sift the flour into the bowl and beat until just combined.

2 Spoon the batter into the prepared cake pan(s), leveling the surface with the back of a spoon. Bake for the recommended time or until the top springs back slightly when gently pressed with a finger and a skewer inserted into the center comes out clean. Oven temperatures can vary, so check on the cake(s) about 5 minutes before the end of the recommended baking time.

3 Remove the cake(s) from the oven and leave to cool 5 minutes, then remove from the pan, transfer to a wire rack and leave to cool completely.

Flavored Sponge Cakes

Cappuccino Sponge: add coffee extract to the mixture after the eggs have been incorporated (before you add the flour).
Chocolate Sponge: use less self-rising flour and add unsweetened cocoa powder to the mixture with the flour.
Citrus Sponge: beat in the finely grated zest of lemons or oranges with the sugar and butter.
Mocha Sponge: add coffee extract to the mixture after the eggs have been incorporated. Use less self-rising flour (see chocolate sponge variation for quantity) and add unsweetened cocoa powder to the mixture with the flour.
Vanilla Sponge: beat in vanilla extract with the sugar and butter.

Use these sponge recipes for the following recipes throughout this book:

**Sugared Rose
Petal Cake**
page 12

**Fresh Flower
Fondant Fancies**
page 18

**Pom Pom
Wedding Cake**
page 60

**Chocolate Heart
Cake Pops**
page 68

Dragon Cake
page 74

**White Blossom
Christening Cake**
page 84

	4in. round or square cake 6 cupcakes	5in. round or square cake	6in. round or square cake 4 x 3¼in. mini ball cake halves 24 mini cupcakes	7in. round or square cake	8in. round, square or heart cake 12 cupcakes	9in round or square cake 2 x 6in. ball cake halves
salted butter	3½ tbsp.	⅓ cup (⅔ stick)	scant ½ cup (¾ stick)	⅔ cup (1⅓ sticks)	1 cup (2 sticks)	1⅓ cups (2⅔ sticks)
superfine sugar	scant ¼ cup	scant ⅓ cup	scant ½ cup	heaped ⅔ cup	scant 1 cup	scant 1⅓ cups
eggs	1 medium	1 large	2 large	3 large	4 large	6 large
self-rising flour	scant ½ cup	heaped ½ cup	heaped ¾ cup	scant 1¼ cups	scant 1⅔ cups	scant 2½ cups
for vanilla sponge cake	¼ tsp. vanilla extract	½ tsp. vanilla extract	½ tsp. vanilla extract	1 tsp. vanilla extract	1 tsp. vanilla extract	1½ tsp. vanilla extract
for chocolate sponge cake	1 tsp. unsweetened cocoa powder	2 tsp. unsweetened cocoa powder	2 tsp. unsweetened cocoa powder	1 tbsp. unsweetened cocoa powder	scant ¼ cup unsweetened cocoa powder	⅓ cup unsweetened cocoa powder
	heaped ⅓ cup self-rising flour	scant ½ cup self-rising flour	¾ cup self-rising flour	heaped 1 cup self-rising flour	scant 1½ cups self-rising	scant 2¼ cups self-rising flour
for citrus sponge cake	zest of ½ lemon or ¼ orange	zest of ½ lemon or ¼ orange	zest of 1 lemon or ½ orange	zest of 2 lemons or 1 orange	zest of 2 lemons or 1 orange	zest of 3 lemons or 1½ oranges
for cappuccino sponge cake	3 tsp. coffee extract	1 tbsp. coffee extract	1–2 tbsp. coffee extract	2 tbsp. coffee extract	3 tbsp. coffee extract	⅓ cup coffee extract
for mocha sponge cake	1 tbsp. coffee extract	1 tbsp. coffee extract	2 tbsp. coffee extract	3 tbsp. coffee extract	¼ cup coffee extract	scant ½ cup coffee extract
	1 tsp. unsweetened cocoa powder	1 tsp. unsweetened cocoa powder	2 tsp. unsweetened cocoa powder	1 tbsp. unsweetened cocoa powder	scant ¼ cup unsweetened cocoa powder	¼ cup unsweetened cocoa powder
baking time	20 minutes for large cakes	25 minutes	30 minutes for large cakes	35 minutes	40 minutes for large cakes	50 minutes for large cakes
	15 minutes for cupcakes		15 minutes for mini ball cake halves		12–15 minutes for cupcakes	40 minutes for ball cake halves
			8 minutes for mini cupcakes			
serves	large cakes: 10	12	large cakes: 15–20	20–30	large cakes: 30–40	large cakes: 50–75
	cupcakes: 6		mini ball cake halves: 4		cupcakes: 12	ball cake halves: 12–16
			mini cupcakes: 24			

Festive Ball Cakes
page 92

Christmas Pudding Cake
page 97

Ivory Corsage Wedding Cake
page 114

Butterfly Fancies
page 116

Teapot Cake
page 122

Flower Cake Pops
page 132

Rose Heart Cookies

MAKES 30 COOKIES
powdered sugar, for dusting
2¾oz. pale green-colored gum
    paste (see pages 160–1)
2¾oz. red-colored gum paste
    (see pages 160–1)
edible glue or 2 tbsp. white
    Royal Icing (see page 46)
30 cookies made using 1 recipe
    quantity Cookie Dough of your
    choice (see pages 26–7), cut
    out with the heart template
    (see page 162) or with a heart
    cookie cutter

YOU WILL NEED
small rolling pin
1in. and 1¼in. veined leaf
    plunger cutters
indented foam pad or a piece
    of crinkled aluminum foil
small single rose mold
small paintbrush
baking sheet, lined with
    parchment paper
small angled metal spatula

HINTS
Working in batches will help you
to keep the size of the roses even.

You will need to make the leaves
and the roses the day before they
are needed.

1 To make the leaves, dust the work surface with a little powdered sugar, then knead the pale green gum paste until it is soft and pliable. Roll out the kneaded gum paste quite thinly and stamp out a leaf using the 1in. veined leaf plunger cutter. While the gum paste is still soft, mold the leaf into a slightly curved shape. Stamping and molding one leaf at a time **(a)**, repeat with the remaining gum paste to make 30 leaves in total, using both the 1in. and 1¼in. veined leaf plunger cutters to create a mixture of sizes. Place the leaves on the indented foam pad—this will help the leaves to keep their curved shape as they dry. Leave to dry overnight, uncovered, in a cool, dry place.

2 To make the roses, dust the work surface with a little more powdered sugar, then knead the red gum paste until it is soft and pliable. Roll a little of the kneaded gum paste into 6 pea-sized balls. Keep the remaining gum paste in an airtight container until needed so it does not dry out and crack. Dust the rose mold with a little powdered sugar to prevent the gum paste from sticking to it. Gently push one of the gum paste balls into the mold, applying even pressure with your thumb to ensure the gum paste picks up all of the detailing **(b)**. Carefully pop the gum paste rose out of the mold. Remove any excess powdered sugar from the rose with the paintbrush, then transfer the rose to the prepared baking sheet with the angled metal spatula. Repeat with the remaining balls of red gum paste to make 6 roses. Working in batches, repeat with the remaining red gum paste to make 30 roses in total. Leave the roses to dry overnight, uncovered, in a cool, dry place.

3 When the gum paste decorations have dried, brush the back of the roses and leaves with a little edible glue, then gently press them onto the top of the cookies to make 30 decorated cookies. Leave the cookies at least 10 to 15 minutes, uncovered, in a cool, dry place to allow the edible glue to set.

(a)   **(b)**

Rose Bouquet Cupcakes

MAKES 6 CUPCAKES
powdered sugar, for dusting
12¾oz. red-colored gum paste
    (see pages 160–1)
edible glue or cooled, boiled
    water
red edible glitter
½ recipe quantity Chocolate
    Frosting (see page 118)
6 Rich Chocolate Cupcakes
    (see page 129), baked in dark
    brown paper baking cups

YOU WILL NEED
small rolling pin
sharp knife
ruler
small paintbrush
baking sheet lined with
    parchment paper
pastry bag with a
    ¾in. closed-star tip
6 pieces of very narrow red
    ribbon (optional)

HINTS
You will need to make the
roses at least a day before
they are needed.

For a softer look, take 6 vanilla
cupcakes baked in white paper
baking cups, cover with high
swirls of vanilla buttercream and
decorate with pale pink roses. Or,
for a jewel-like effect, use orange,
pink, aqua or lime glittered roses.

1 This recipe makes six cupcakes but if you want to make only one, simply use one-sixth of each of the listed ingredients. Dust the work surface with a little powdered sugar, then knead 4¼oz. of the gum paste until it is soft and pliable. Roll out the kneaded gum paste quite thinly, then cut into strips, each about ⅝ x 2½in. Roll the trimmings into a ball, then reroll until quite thin and continue to cut into strips. Repeat until all of the gum paste is used up.

2 To make a rose, take one of the gum paste strips and roll the end of the paintbrush along one of the long edges, pressing gently to avoid tearing it, to create the frill at the top of the petals **(a)**. Brush a little water along the three plain edges of the strip. With the frilled-side facing inward, gently roll up the strip to form a rose **(b)**. Pinch the gum paste together at the bottom of the rose, then cut off the excess gum paste to form a flat base. Transfer the finished rose to the prepared baking sheet. Repeat step 2 with the remaining gum paste strips to make about 35 roses. Working in batches, repeat with the remaining gum paste to make approximately 100 roses in total, dusting the work surface with powdered sugar as necessary. Leave the roses to dry overnight, uncovered, in a cool, dry place.

3 When the roses have dried, brush 5 to 10 roses with a little edible glue. Dip the end of a teaspoon in edible glitter, then holding the spoon in one hand, gently tap the handle with the other to lightly dust the roses with glitter **(c)**. Working in small batches, repeat until all the roses have been dusted with glitter. Pour any excess glitter on the parchment paper back into the pot.

4 Spoon the chocolate frosting into the pastry bag and pipe a high swirl onto one of the cupcakes (see page 157). Arrange 15 to 16 of the roses in a single layer over the cupcake to cover the frosting. Wrap a piece of red ribbon around the base of the cupcake and finish with a bow, if you like. Repeat with the remaining frosting, cupcakes, roses and ribbon, if you like, to make six decorated cupcakes.

(a)

(b)

(c)

Chocolate Heart Cake Pops

MAKES 30 CAKE POPS
8in. Basic Sponge Cake
  (see pages 62–3)
¾ recipe quantity Vanilla
  Frosting (see page 118)
1lb. 5oz. chocolate confectionery
  coating

YOU WILL NEED
parchment paper
2in. heart cookie cutter
30 paper lollipop sticks
6 x 20in. multicolored or
  patterned ribbons, ½in. wide
  and cut into 5 equal lengths
  (optional)

HINTS
Baking the sponge cake the day before you make the cake pops will make the mixture easier to crumble.

Confectionery coating (also called candy coating) is widely available online. You can buy it in various colors and in a variety of flavors, including dark, milk and white chocolate. Confectionery coating is easy to use because, unlike chocolate, it does not need to be tempered. Heating and cooling chocolate without controlling the temperature (tempering) causes blemishes to appear on the surface. The chocolate will also crumble rather than snap.

1 Put the cake in a mixing bowl and crumble it with your fingers until it resembles coarse breadcrumbs. Make sure there are no large pieces of sponge cake left in the bowl because this will make the cake pops lumpy. Add the frosting and gently stir to form a moist cake mixture. To test if the mixture is the correct consistency for molding, take a small amount of mixture and gently press it into a ball shape **(a)**—if the mixture holds its shape, it is ready to use.

2 Set a sheet of parchment paper on the work surface and place the 2in. heart cookie cutter on top. Take a little of the cake pop mixture and press it into the cutter to form a smooth base, then use your fingers to mold a smooth, curved front **(b)**. Carefully remove the molded mixture from the cutter and repeat to make 30 heart-shaped cake pops. Chill the cake pops in the refrigerator about 1 hour until firm. Alternatively, freeze the cake pops about 15 minutes until firm.

3 Put the confectionery coating in a heatproof bowl and rest it over a saucepan of gently simmering water, making sure the bottom of the bowl does not touch the water. Heat, stirring occasionally, until melted. Alternatively, put the confectionery coating in a bowl and microwave, uncovered, on medium 2 minutes until melted, stirring every 30 seconds to ensure the coating does not overheat. The confectionery coating should have a smooth pouring consistency similar to heavy cream.

4 Dip the tip of one of the lollipop sticks about ½in. into the melted confectionery coating and then gently push it into the bottom of one of the cake pops until the coated tip is hidden from view. Holding the end of the lollipop stick, gently twist the cake pop through the confectionery coating **(c)** until it is completely coated, using a teaspoon to help if necessary. Lift the cake pop out of the confectionery coating, allowing any excess coating to fall back into the bowl. Transfer the coated cake pop to a drinking glass, with the cake-pop end upward, and leave to set 10 to 15 minutes. Repeat with the remaining cake pops and lollipop sticks, reheating the confectionery coating if necessary, to make 30 coated cake pops. When the confectionery coating has completely set, tie a ribbon around each lollipop stick just below the cake pop and finish with a bow, if you like.

(a)

(b)

(c)

CHAPTER THREE

**Seasonal events and birthdays provide plenty
of opportunities to be creative. My favorite time of year
is undoubtedly Christmas, when baking and decorating can be
even more extravagant than usual. For a spectacular Christmas
centerpiece, try the Gingerbread House or the Christmas
Pudding Cake. If you need to plan an unforgettable children's
birthday party, just invite along the Party Penguins.
Let the celebrations begin!**

DECORATE
TO
CELEBRATE

Christmas Wreath Tree Decorations

MAKES 12 COOKIES
¾ cup green-colored stiff-peak
 Royal Icing (see page 46)
12 cookies made using ¾ recipe
 quantity Cookie Dough of your
 choice (see pages 26–7), cut
 out with the wreath template
 (see page 165)
¼ cup red-colored stiff-peak
 Royal Icing (see page 46)

YOU WILL NEED
pastry bag with a small leaf tip
 attached
pastry bag with a no. 2 plain tip
 attached
13ft. gold ribbon, ¼in. wide,
 cut into 24 equal lengths

HINTS
If you don't have a small leaf
tip, snipping a small triangle at
the pointed end of a disposable
pastry bag creates a similar effect.

To achieve the leaf effect with
a pastry bag, gently squeeze a
small amount of royal icing out of
the bag and when the leaf is the
correct size, carefully pull the tip
up and away from the icing.
If the leaves are not holding their
shape, your royal icing might not
be stiff enough. Simply mix in a
little more powdered sugar before
piping again. Repeat if necessary.

1 Spoon the green stiff-peak royal icing into the pastry bag with the small leaf tip attached to it. Decorating one cookie at a time, pipe rows of leaves onto each cookie starting from the inside edge and working your way toward the outer edge **(a)**. (For hints on piping, see pages 157–9.) When the cookie is covered in leaves, pipe a few more leaves over the top to fill any gaps, if necessary. Repeat with the remaining cookies and green stiff-peak royal icing to make 12 decorated cookies in total. Leave 15 minutes, uncovered, in a cool, dry place to allow the royal icing to set.

2 When the royal icing has set, spoon the red stiff-peak royal icing into the pastry bag with the no. 2 plain tip attached to it. For the holly berries, pipe tiny dots of red icing onto the green leaves on each cookie. Leave the cookies overnight, uncovered, in a cool, dry place to allow the decoration to set completely.

3 When the cookies have completely set, take a piece of gold ribbon and carefully thread it through the hole in the cookie, then tie a bow at the top of the cookie. Carefully thread another piece of ribbon underneath the ribbon at the back of the bow and tie in a loop (see picture). Repeat with the remaining cookies and ribbons to make 12 hanging tree decorations.

(a)

Dragon Cake

MAKES 1 CAKE
powdered sugar, for dusting
5½oz. blue-colored modeling
    paste (see pages 160–1)
2¼oz. green-colored modeling
    paste (see pages 160–1)
2 x 8in. round Basic Sponge
    Cakes (see pages 62–3)
1 recipe quantity Vanilla
    Buttercream (see page 16)
⅓ cup seedless raspberry jam
1lb. 12oz. white gum paste
    (see pages 160–1)
7oz. red-colored gum paste
    (see pages 160–1)
edible glue or cooled, boiled
    water
⅛oz. black-colored gum paste
    (see pages 160–1)

YOU WILL NEED
small rolling pin
¼in. marzipan spacers
    (optional)
sharp knife
dragon and flame templates
    (see page 164)
baking sheet lined with
    parchment paper
8in. round cake board
small paintbrush
ruler

HINTS
You will need to make the dragon
parts at least a day before you are
ready to assemble the cake.

You can change the expression
of the dragon by altering the
position of the pupil.

1 Dust the work surface with a little powdered sugar, then knead the blue modeling paste until it is soft and pliable. Roll out the kneaded modeling paste until it is ¼in. thick, using marzipan spacers, if you like, and cut out the dragon's head, ears, body and legs, using the templates. Indent the toes and mouth with the sharp knife, then smooth the edges of all the parts with your fingers. Repeat with the green modeling paste to make the tummy and wings, indenting the line details on both parts with the sharp knife and smoothing the edges with your fingers. Without assembling the dragon, transfer the parts to the prepared baking sheet and leave to dry overnight, uncovered, in a cool, dry place. Roll the trimmings into balls and store in an airtight container to prevent them from drying out.

2 When the dragon parts have dried, following the instructions on page 150 and, using the cake board as a firm base, layer the sponge cakes, then fill with buttercream and jam to make one tall 8in. cake. Following the instructions on page 152, cover the cake with the remaining buttercream. Chill in the refrigerator 2 hours. When the buttercream has set, dust the work surface with a little powdered sugar, then knead the white gum paste until it is soft and pliable. Following the instructions on page 153, cover the cake with the kneaded gum paste. Roll the trimmings into a ball and store in an airtight container so the gum paste does not dry out and crack.

3 Dust the work surface with powdered sugar, then knead half of the red gum paste until it is soft and pliable. Roll out the kneaded gum paste quite thinly and cut out about 10 flames, using the template. Brush the back of each flame with edible glue, then press them vertically onto the side of the cake (see picture). Repeat with the remaining red gum paste until the side of the cake is covered in flames.

4 Brush the back of the dragon's body and head with a little edible glue, then attach them to the top of the cake. Using the picture as a guide, attach the ears, tummy, legs and wings, securing each part with edible glue. To make the nose, roll a tiny ball of blue modeling paste, then flatten it slightly and indent with the end of the paintbrush. To make the eye, roll a very small ball of the remaining white gum paste. For the pupil, roll a tiny ball of black gum paste and attach it to the eye, then attach an even tinier ball of white gum paste to the top of the pupil, flattening it slightly as you do so. Attach the nose and eye to the head with edible glue. To make the tail, roll the remaining blue modeling paste into a long, tapered sausage about 6in. in length. Flatten the wider end of the sausage to form the root of the tail, then attach it to the top of the cake with edible glue, making sure it lines up squarely with the body. Mold a tiny ball of green modeling paste into a triangle and attach it to the tip of the tail with edible glue. Curl the end of the tail slightly to form an s-shape over the top and side of the cake, securing it in place with edible glue. Roll the remaining green modeling paste into tiny balls, then attach them to the body and head of the dragon with edible glue, flattening them slightly as you do so. Leave the cake overnight to allow the gum and modeling pastes to dry.

Marble Cake

VANILLA SPONGE CAKE
salted butter
superfine sugar
vanilla extract
egg(s)
self-rising flour

CHOCOLATE SPONGE
CAKE
salted butter
dark brown sugar
egg(s)
unsweetened cocoa powder
self-rising flour

YOU WILL NEED
electric mixer
cake pan(s) lined with
  parchment paper (for hints on
  lining cake pans, see page 149)

HINT
If the cake is going to be split into layers, wrap it in parchment paper and aluminum foil, then leave it to rest overnight to firm up a little. This will make it easier to cut. (For hints on layering, filling and covering cakes, see pages 150 and 152–3.)

The table opposite shows you the quantity of ingredients and baking times required for different cake sizes and styles. It also offers advice on serving portions. Simply select your size and style and follow the method below.

1 Preheat the oven to 350°F and allow the butter for the vanilla and chocolate sponge cakes to soften slightly. For the vanilla sponge cake, put the softened butter, sugar and vanilla extract in a mixing bowl and beat with the electric mixer until light and fluffy. Lightly beat the egg(s), then gradually add to the mixture. If it starts to curdle, add a little bit of the flour. Sift the flour into the bowl, then beat until just combined.

2 For the chocolate sponge cake, put the softened butter and dark brown sugar in a clean mixing bowl and beat with the electric mixer until light and fluffy. Lightly beat the egg(s), then gradually add them to the mixture. If it starts to curdle, add a little bit of the flour. Sift the unsweetened cocoa powder and flour into the bowl, then beat until just combined.

3 Using 2 large spoons, drop alternate spoonfuls of the vanilla and chocolate cake batters into the prepared pan(s) until both mixtures have been used. Cut through the batters several times with a knife to create a marbled effect. If necessary, level the surface with the back of a spoon, taking care not to spoil the marbled effect. Bake for the recommended time or until the top springs back slightly when gently pressed with a finger and a skewer inserted into the center comes out clean. Oven temperatures can vary, so check on the cake(s) about 5 minutes before the end of the recommended baking time.

4 Remove the cake(s) from the oven and leave to cool 10 minutes, then remove from the pan, transfer to a wire rack and leave to cool completely.

Use this marble cake recipe for the following recipes throughout this book:

Valentine Cigarillo Cake
page 48

Festive Ball Cakes
page 92

Christmas Pudding Cake
page 97

Gift-Wrapped Cake
page 135

Daisy Chain Mouse Cake
page 136

	4in. round or square cake 6 cupcakes	5in. round or square cake	6in. round or square cake 4 x 3in. mini ball cake halves 24 mini cupcakes	7in. round or square cake	8in. round, square or heart cake 12 cupcakes	9in. round or square cake 2 x 6in. ball cake halves
VANILLA SPONGE CAKE:						
salted butter	heaped 1½ tbsp.	heaped 1½ tbsp.	3½ tbsp.	⅓ cup (⅔ stick)	scant ½ cup (¾ stick)	⅔ cup (1⅓ sticks)
superfine sugar	1 tbsp. plus 2 tsp.	1 tbsp. plus 2 tsp.	scant ¼ cup	scant ⅓ cup	scant ½ cup	scant ⅔ cup
vanilla extract	½ tsp.	½ tsp.	1 tsp.	1½ tsp.	2 tsp.	1 tbsp.
eggs	1 small	1 small	1 large	1 large	2 large	3 large
self-rising flour	scant ¼ cup	scant ¼ cup	scant ½ cup	heaped ½ cup	heaped ¾ cup	scant 1¼ cups
CHOCOLATE SPONGE CAKE:						
salted butter	heaped 1½ tbsp.	heaped 1½ tbsp.	3½ tbsp.	⅓ cup (⅔ stick)	scant ½ cup (¾ stick)	⅔ cup (1⅓ sticks)
dark brown sugar	1 tbsp. plus 2 tsp.	1 tbsp. plus 2 tsp.	heaped ¼ cup	heaped ⅓ cup	heaped ½ cup	heaped ¾ cup
eggs	1 small	1 small	1 large	1 large	2 large	3 large
unsweetened cocoa powder	2 tsp.	2 tsp.	scant ¼ cup	¼ cup	⅓ cup	½ cup
self-rising flour	1 tbsp.	1 tbsp.	¼ cup	heaped ⅓ cup	½ cup	¾ cup
baking time	20 minutes for large cakes	25 minutes	30 minutes for large cakes	40 minutes for large cakes	45 minutes for large cakes	50 minutes
	15 minutes for cupcakes		15 minutes for mini ball cake halves		15 minutes for cupcakes	45 minutes for ball cake halves
			8 minutes for mini cupcakes			
serves	large cakes: 10	12	large cakes: 15–20	20–30	large cakes: 30–40	large cakes: 40–50
	cupcakes: 6		mini ball cake halves: 4			ball cake halves: 12–16
			mini cupcakes: 24		cupcakes: 12	

Gingerbread House

MAKES 1 HOUSE
1 recipe quantity Gingerbread Dough (see page 27)
powdered sugar, for dusting
3½oz. caramel-colored gum paste (see pages 160–1)
2¼oz. red-colored gum paste (see pages 160–1)
1lb. 13oz. white gum paste (see pages 160–1)
½ cup white soft-peak Royal Icing (see page 46)
½ cup white stiff-peak Royal Icing (see page 46)

YOU WILL NEED
rolling pin
gingerbread house templates (see page 166)
sharp knife
scallop-edge cutter (optional)
2 baking sheets lined with parchment paper
ruler
2 pastry bags, 1 with a no. 2 plain tip attached
9in. square cake board
39in. white ribbon, ³⁄₈in. wide
straight frill cutter (optional)

HINT
You will need to make the walls and roof panels of the gingerbread house, door, candy cane and heart decorations the day before they are needed.

1 Preheat the oven to 350˚F. Roll out the gingerbread dough following the instructions on page 148. Place the templates for the walls and roof panels on the dough and cut around them with the sharp knife. You will need 2 side walls, 2 end walls and 2 roof panels. (For hints on cutting out cookies, see page 148.)

2 Indent a tiled pattern onto the roof panels with the scallop-edge cutter. Alternatively, score the pattern with the sharp knife. If you would like your house to have a window, position the heart-shaped template on one of the end walls and cut around it—this will be the back of the house. Using a metal spatula, transfer the walls and roof panels to the prepared baking sheets, spacing the cookies well apart. Cook 14 minutes, then remove from the oven. The cooking time is slightly longer than usual because the cookies need to be firm to give the house rigidity. Transfer the cookies to a wire rack and leave to cool completely, then store in an airtight container.

3 Dust the work surface with powdered sugar, then knead ¾oz. of the caramel gum paste and 1¾oz. each of the red and white gum pastes until they are soft and pliable. For the door, roll out the caramel gum paste quite thinly and cut out a door, using the template. Score a cross-hatched pattern onto the front of the door using the sharp knife. Leave to dry overnight, uncovered, in a cool, dry place.

4 Dust the work surface with a little more powdered sugar. For the candy cane decorations, roll about ½oz. each of the kneaded red and white gum pastes into 2 long thin sausages. Twist the colors together, then gently roll them on the work surface **(a)** to form one long candy cane strip. Twist the strip again to form a tight candy cane. Repeat with the remaining kneaded red and white gum pastes. Take the candy canes and cut a length about 5½in. and mold it around the door to form an arch; cut 4 corner poles, each about 1½in., and mold the remaining canes into 4 lollipop swirls. Roll out the remaining red gum paste quite thinly and cut out 2 hearts, using the template. If your house has a window, you only need to cut out 1 heart. Leave all the decorations to dry overnight, uncovered, in a cool, dry place **(b)**.

(a)

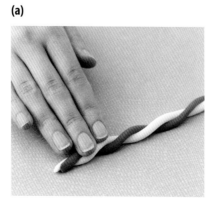

(b)

(c)

5 When the door and decorations have dried, decorate the walls of the house. Spoon the soft-peak royal icing into the pastry bag that has the no. 2 plain tip attached to it. Secure the door and candy cane arch to the bottom of a (plain) end wall panel with a little royal icing—this will be the front of the house. Attach one of the red hearts about 1in. above the door, using royal icing. If your house does not have a window, attach the other red heart in the same position to the back end wall of the house. Attach 2 candy cane lollipop swirls to each of the side walls using royal icing.

6 When all the decorations are attached, pipe a large dot of soft-peak royal icing onto the door for a handle. Next, pipe the detail on the red hearts and a little fleur de lys above them (or above the window), then pipe curly lines onto the end and side walls. (For hints on piping, see pages 157–9). Set the walls to one side and allow to dry thoroughly **(c)**. Do not try to assemble the house while the decorations are still wet.

7 When the decorations have dried, spoon the stiff-peak royal icing into the remaining pastry bag, then snip off the pointed end if necessary. Working quickly, take the front end wall and pipe some royal icing onto the inside of the side edges, then place the side walls in position **(d)**. Repeat with the back end wall and place in position, then support the wall panels with drinking glasses and leave to dry overnight in a cool, dry place **(e)**. Store the pastry bag in an airtight container until needed.

8 Meanwhile, dust the work surface with a little more powdered sugar, then knead 1lb. 9oz. of the white gum paste until it is soft and pliable. Following the instructions on page 154, cover the cake board with gum paste and line the edge with white ribbon. Leave to set overnight, uncovered, in a cool, dry place.

(d)

(e)

9 When the walls have dried, pipe some stiff-peak royal icing along the roof edges and place the roof panels in position **(f and g)**. Hold the roof panels in position **(h)**, then support the lower roof edges with drinking glasses to stop the roof panels from slipping down. Leave to dry a few hours, or ideally overnight. Store the pastry bag in an airtight container.

10 When the house is stable and all the elements are secure, pipe a little stiff-peak royal icing onto the bottom edge of each wall panel and carefully place the house onto the center of the covered cake board. Attach the candy cane poles to the corners of the house with a little more royal icing **(i)**. For the gable ends, roll out the remaining caramel gum paste quite thinly and stamp out 4 decorative borders, each one about 5½ x ¾in., using the straight frill cutter. Alternatively, cut out a decorative border design by hand with the sharp knife. Pipe some royal icing onto the edges of the roof and attach the borders along each gable **(j)**, trimming as necessary.

11 For the roof snow, roll out the remaining white gum paste quite thinly and cut out a 6¼ x 3½in. rectangle, then reroll the trimmings and cut out 2 more rectangles, each about 6¼ x 2in. Cut curvy edges down the sides of each rectangle. Attach the large piece of snow over the ridge of the roof **(k)**, and the smaller pieces to the bottom edges with royal icing. Leave to dry.

(f)   **(g)**   **(h)**

(i)   **(j)**   **(k)**

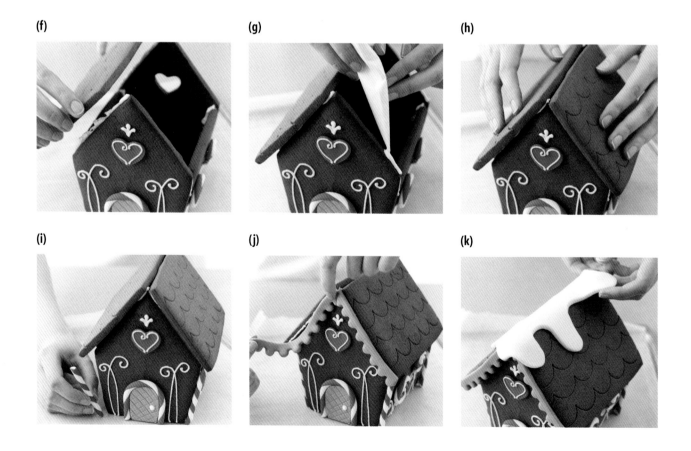

Thanksgiving Cookies

MAKES 12 COOKIES
powdered sugar, for dusting
8oz. pale green-colored gum
   paste (see pages 160–1)
12 cookies made using ½ recipe
   quantity Cookie Dough of your
   choice (see pages 26–7), cut
   out with the circle template
   (see page 167) or a 2½in. plain
   round cookie cutter
edible glue or 2 tbsp. apricot
   jam, warmed
8oz. ivory-colored gum paste
   (see pages 160–1)
¼ cup ivory-colored soft-peak
   Royal Icing (see page 46)
¼ cup light green-colored soft-
   peak Royal Icing (see page 46)

YOU WILL NEED
small rolling pin
2¼in. or 2½in. plain round
   cookie cutter
small paintbrushes
small angled metal spatula
Thanksgiving leaf designs
   (see page 167)
sheet of 8 x 11in. paper
straight pins
scriber or sharp needle
2 pastry bags, each with a
   no. 2 plain tip attached

HINTS
Scribing is a little like creating
a "join the dots" puzzle. It's really
worth taking time and care over
because the indentations made
by the scriber will act as your
piping guide. Detailed scribing
will result in a delicate finish.
Always allow the gum paste to
harden slightly before scribing.

The textured effect created by
piping and dragging the icing
over the cookie is called "brush
embroidery." You can use this
technique on any cookie or cake
that's covered in gum paste.

1 Dust the work surface with a little powdered sugar, then knead the pale green gum paste until it is soft and pliable. Roll out the kneaded gum paste quite thinly and stamp out 6 circles with the 2¼in. circle cutter. Brush the surface of half of the cookies with edible glue. Using the angled metal spatula, place the gum paste circles onto the prepared cookies, taking care not to stretch or pull the gum paste, then lightly smooth down each circle with your fingers. Repeat with the ivory gum paste, remaining cookies and edible glue to make 12 gum paste-coated cookies in total. Leave the gum paste coating to harden slightly at least 2 hours, uncovered, in a cool, dry place.

2 Meanwhile, trace each of the leaf designs onto the sheet of paper. Closely cut around the outline of each one to make four scribing guides. When the gum paste coating has hardened slightly, place a scribing guide on top of one of the cookies. Secure the guide in place with a couple of pins, pushing them through the top and bottom points of the leaf design—if the guide moves during scribing, the leaf design will be messy and hard to pipe over. Support the edge of the cookie with one hand, then lightly prick the outline and vein details of the leaf design onto the cookie with the scriber **(a)**. Repeat with the remaining cookies, using each of the scribing guides three times.

3 To decorate the pale green cookies, spoon the ivory soft-peak royal icing into one of the pastry bags and dampen a paintbrush with a little water. Using the indentations made by the scriber as a guide, pipe a line of royal icing over one-quarter of the leaf outline, then lightly drag the icing toward the center of the cookie with the dampened paintbrush to create a textured effect **(b)**. (For hints on piping, see pages 157–9.) Working in sections, continue to pipe and drag the icing toward the center of the cookie until you have completed the outline of the leaf. Carefully pipe the vein details on top, using the indentations you made with the scriber as a guide. Decorating one cookie at a time and dampening the paintbrush as necessary, repeat with the remaining ivory soft-peak royal icing and pale green cookies. Repeat step 3 with the light-green soft-peak royal icing and ivory cookies to make 12 decorated cookies in total. Leave the cookies overnight, uncovered, in a cool, dry place to allow the royal icing to set.

(a)

(b)

White Blossom Christening Cake

MAKES 1 CAKE
7in. round Basic Sponge Cake
  (see pages 62–3)
5in. round Citrus Sponge Cake
  (see pages 62–3)
1 recipe quantity Vanilla
  Buttercream (see page 16)
powdered sugar, for dusting
2lb. 4oz. pale blue-colored gum
  paste (see pages 160–1)
3½oz. white gum paste
  (see pages 160–1)
½ cup white soft-peak Royal
  Icing (see page 46)

YOU WILL NEED
7in. round cake board
5in. round cake board
small rolling pin
½in. and 1in. blossom
  plunger cutters
indented foam pad or a piece
  of crinkled aluminum foil
double-ended ball tool
  (optional)
plastic dowel rods
2 pastry bags, 1 with a
  no. 2 plain tip attached

1 Following the instructions on page 150 and using the cake boards as firm bases, layer the sponge cakes, then fill with buttercream. Following the instructions on page 152, cover the cakes with the remaining buttercream. Chill in the refrigerator 2 hours. When the buttercream has set, dust the work surface with a little powdered sugar, then knead 1lb. 9oz. of the pale blue gum paste until it is soft and pliable. Following the instructions on page 153, cover the 7in. cake with the kneaded gum paste. Repeat with the remaining gum paste to cover the 5in. cake. Roll the gum paste trimmings into a ball and store in an airtight container until needed.

2 Dust the work surface with a little more powdered sugar, then knead the white gum paste until it is soft and pliable. Roll out the kneaded gum paste quite thinly and stamp out 30–40 blossoms using the ½in. blossom plunger cutter **(a)**. Place the blossoms on the indented foam pad, then indent the center of each one with the small head of the ball tool or with the tip of your little finger **(b)**. Roll the trimmings into a ball and repeat with the 1in. blossom plunger cutter to make 25–30 blossoms, indenting the center of each one with the large head of the ball tool or with your little finger. Leave the cakes and the blossoms overnight, uncovered, in a cool, dry place to allow the gum paste and blossoms to dry.

3 When the gum paste and the blossoms have dried, follow the instructions on page 156 and stack the 5in. cake on top of the 7in. cake with plastic dowel rods. For a clean join between the tiers, put a little pale blue gum paste in a small bowl. Add water, a few drops at a time, and mix until a thick paste forms. Spoon the paste into the pastry bag that does not have a tip attached, and snip off the end if necessary. Pipe the paste around the bottom of the top tier, then run your finger along the join to remove any excess paste. (For hints on piping, see pages 157–9.) Spoon the royal icing into the pastry bag with the no. 2 plain tip attached. Pipe 6 dots in the center of the large blossoms **(c)** to form a blossom shape (see picture) and a single dot in the center of the small blossoms. Attach the blossoms on top and down the sides of the cake, securing each one with a dot of royal icing. Leave to set, uncovered, in a cool, dry place, before serving.

(a)

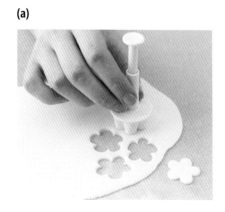

(b)

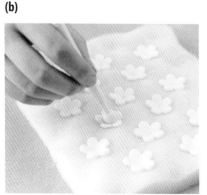

(c)

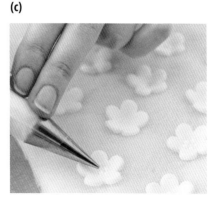

Party Penguins

MAKES 6 PENGUINS
2 tsp. salted butter
1 cup marshmallows
    (pink, white or mixed)
2 dashes of vanilla extract
3½ cups crisped rice cereal
powdered sugar, for dusting
7oz. black-colored gum paste
    (see pages 160–1)
2¼oz. orange-colored gum
    paste (see pages 160–1)
edible glue or cooled, boiled
    water
1¾oz. white gum paste
    (see pages 160–1)
¼oz. each of red-, pink-, pale
    pink- and green-colored gum
    pastes (see pages 160–1)
⅛oz. yellow-colored gum paste
    (see pages 160–1)

YOU WILL NEED
small rolling pin
sharp knife
1in., 1⅓. and ¼in. circle cutters
small paintbrush
ruler
straight frill cutter (optional)

HINT
For quick, easy and delicious
treats, press the marshmallow
mixture into an even layer in a
shallow pan lined with parchment
paper. Leave to cool about 30
minutes and then cut out shapes
with cookie cutters.

1 In a large, heavy-based saucepan, melt the butter over low heat, then add the marshmallows and stir frequently until melted. Remove from the heat. Add the vanilla extract and the crisped rice cereal and stir until combined. Leave to cool slightly 10 minutes.

2 Divide the marshmallow mixture into 6 equal lumps to make 6 bodies. Mold each into a tear-drop shape—you can be firm when handling the mixture. Press each shape to form as smooth a surface as possible **(a)**, because any large bumps will be visible under the gum-paste covering. Mold the bottom of each one into a flat base.

3 Dust the work surface with a little powdered sugar, then knead about 1¾oz. of the black gum paste until it is soft and pliable. Roll out the gum paste quite thinly and use it to cover one of the marshmallow bodies, smoothing down the sides with your hands. Trim off any excess gum paste at the base of the body **(b)**. Repeat with the remaining gum paste, rerolling the trimmings as necessary, until all of the marshmallow bodies are covered. Roll the trimmings into a ball and store in an airtight container so the gum paste does not dry out and crack.

4 For the feet, roll out the orange gum paste quite thinly and cut out 12 circles with the 1in. circle cutter. For toes, indent two small lines on the end of each foot with the end of the paintbrush **(c)**. Place two of the feet side by side and flatten the back half with your thumb to make a flat base for the body to rest on. To attach, brush the flattened sides of the feet with a little edible glue and carefully place a penguin body on top **(d)**. Repeat until all the feet are attached. Roll the trimmings into a ball and store in an airtight container so the gum paste does not dry out and crack.

5 For the flippers, reroll the remaining black gum paste and cut out 6 circles using the 1in. circle cutter. Cut each one in half to make 12 semicircles and attach 2 semicircles, cut-side forward, to each penguin with edible glue **(e).** You can vary the penguins by changing the position of their flippers. For attached flippers, cover the underside of each flipper with edible glue before attaching. For hanging flippers, cover only the top half of each flipper in edible glue. Roll the trimmings into a ball.

(a)   **(b)**

   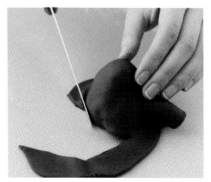

6 For the white tummies, roll out the white gum paste quite thinly and cut out 6 circles using the 1⅓in. circle cutter. Brush a little edible glue onto one of the tummies and attach it to a penguin, positioning it slightly nearer the feet to leave space for the penguin's face **(f)**. Repeat until all the tummies are attached. Roll the trimmings into a ball and store in an airtight container so the gum paste does not dry out and crack.

7 Divide the remaining orange gum paste into 6 large pea-sized balls and shape each one into a cone for the beaks. Secure each beak in place with a little edible glue **(g)**.

8 For the eyes, roll 12 very small balls out of the remaining white gum paste. Put a little edible glue on the back of each one and push the eyes gently into position just above the beak, flattening them slightly as you do so. For pupils, roll out 12 tiny balls from the remaining black gum paste and secure each one in place with a little edible glue. You can change the expression of each penguin by altering the position of the pupils **(h)**.

(c)   **(d)**   **(e)**

(f)   **(g)**   **(h)**

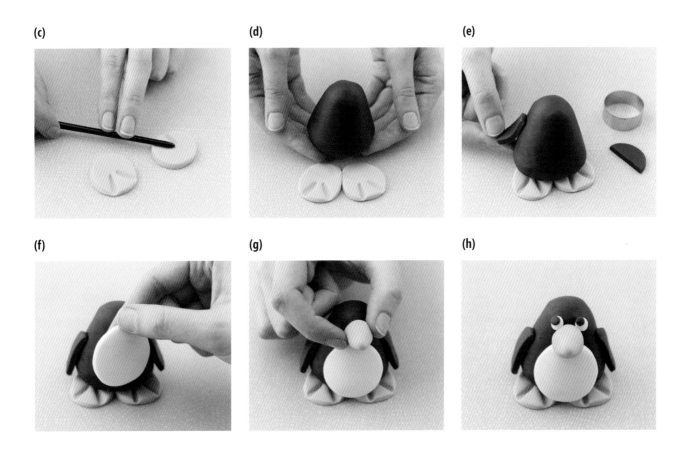

9 Make a selection of hats and outfits using the red, pink, pale pink, green and yellow gum pastes and any leftover scraps of gum-paste trimmings. Knead all the gum pastes until they are soft and pliable and roll out each one quite thinly.

For a hat, cut out a 4 x ⅝in. rectangle of gum paste in any color. Cut a decorative border along one long edge using the straight frill cutter or the sharp knife. Wrap the gum paste around the penguin's head to form a hat, conceal the join at the back, and secure with a little edible glue.

For a superhero mask, cut out a 4 x ⅝in. rectangle of gum paste in any color. Trim the edge so that it is wider in the middle section and tapers off at both ends (see picture). Cut out 2 eye holes using the ¼in. circle cutter. Position the mask over the penguin's eyes and secure in place with edible glue.

For a clown's nose, push a large, pea-sized ball of red gum paste onto the penguin's beak and secure in place with a little edible glue if necessary.

For a sheriff's badge, cut out a small, yellow gum-paste star using the sharp knife and attach to the penguin's body with a little edible glue.

For the bunny rabbit headband, roll 2 large pea-sized balls of white gum paste and mold each one into a flattened tear-drop shape for the ears. For the centers, roll 2 small pea-sized balls of pale pink gum paste and roll each one into a sausage. Flatten the centers and attach each one to the ears with a little edible glue. For the headband, take a little more white gum paste and roll it out into a thin sausage about 2½in long. Flatten the headband and attach it to the top of the penguin's head, trimming as necessary, then place the bunny ears in position, securing both with a little edible glue.

10 Leave the penguins overnight, uncovered, in a cool, dry place to allow the gum paste to dry.

Mini Ghost Cakes

MAKES 6 CAKES
6 Rich Chocolate Cupcakes (see page 129), paper baking cups removed
¼ recipe quantity Vanilla Buttercream (see page 16)
1 recipe quantity Vanilla Sugar Syrup (see page 119)
2 tbsp. seedless raspberry jam
powdered sugar, for dusting
2lb. 4oz. white gum paste (see pages 160–1)
edible glue or cooled, boiled water
1oz. black-colored gum paste (see pages 160–1)

YOU WILL NEED
small serrated knife
6 x 3in. round cake boards
pastry brush
small angled metal spatula
small rolling pin
5in. round circle cutter
¼in. marzipan spacers (optional)
small paintbrush

HINT
You can change the expressions of the ghosts by altering the position of the pupils and changing the shape of the mouth.

1 Using the serrated knife, carefully trim the domed tops off of each cupcake—this will create a flat, stable base for the ghost cakes. Reserve the domed tops. Turn the cupcakes upside down, spread the flat base with a little buttercream and attach to a cake board.

2 Lightly brush the top and side of each cupcake with a little sugar syrup. Using the angled metal spatula, spread a thin layer of buttercream, followed by a layer of jam, on top of each cupcake, then place the reserved domes on top, trimming as necessary to create a neat dome shape. Clean the angled metal spatula, then use it to cover each cupcake with the remaining buttercream. Chill in the refrigerator 2 hours until set.

3 Dust the work surface with a little powdered sugar, then knead half of the white gum paste until it is soft and pliable. Roll out the kneaded gum paste quite thinly and stamp out 6 circles with the 5in. circle cutter. Following the instructions on page 153, cover the cupcakes with gum paste.

4 Dust the work surface with a little more powdered sugar, then knead the remaining white gum paste until it is soft and pliable. Roll out the kneaded gum paste until it is ¼in. thick, using marzipan spacers if you like, and stamp out 6 more circles with the 5in. round circle cutter. Roll over each circle with a small rolling pin to make the gum paste slightly thinner. Brush the top of each cupcake with a little edible glue, then carefully drape a circle of gum paste over the top of each one, pinching it into fabric-like folds at the base. Roll the trimmings into a ball and store in an airtight container so the gum paste does not dry out and crack.

5 Knead the black gum paste until it is soft and pliable. To make the eyes, roll 12 small balls of black gum paste, then slightly flatten each one with your thumb. For the pupils, roll 12 tiny balls of white gum paste and attach them to the eyes with a little edible glue, flattening them slightly as you do so. To make the mouths, roll 6 pea-sized balls of black gum paste into small sausages, then mold and flatten each one into a different shape, trimming the gum paste with a small sharp knife if necessary. Attach the eyes and a mouth to each ghost cake with a little edible glue. Leave the cakes at least 2 hours, uncovered, in a cool, dry place to allow them to set.

Festive Ball Cakes

**MAKES 2 FESTIVE
BALL CAKES**
butter, for greasing
sponge cake batter of your
    choice for 4 x 3¼in. mini ball
    cake halves (see pages 56–7,
    62–3 or 76–7)
1 recipe quantity Sugar Syrup
    (see page 119)
½ recipe quantity Vanilla
    Buttercream (see page 16)
powdered sugar, for dusting
4½oz. red-colored gum paste
    (see pages 160–1)
4½oz. orange-colored gum
    paste (see pages 160–1)

YOU WILL NEED
6 x 3¼in.-cup ball cake pan
long serrated knife
pastry brush
small angled metal spatula
small rolling pin
¼in. marzipan spacers
    (optional)
sharp knife
icing smoother

HINT
Try making these small ball
cakes out of chocolate sponge
cake filled with orange citrus
buttercream (see pages 62–3
and 16).

1 Lightly grease 4 cups of the ball cake pan with butter, then pour the cake batter into the cups until about two-thirds full. Using the back of a metal spoon, form a dip in the center of each cake, pushing the mixture out toward the edges—this prevents the cakes from rising too much in the middle.

2 Bake 15 minutes or until a skewer inserted into the center of each cake comes out clean. Remove from the oven and leave in the pan to cool completely.

3 Level the surface of any cakes that have risen above the top of the pan with the serrated knife, then invert the cakes out of the pan onto a work surface

4 Using the serrated knife, level the flat side of 2 ball cake halves to ensure they will create a neat ball shape when held together. Lightly brush the cut sides of the cakes with some of the sugar syrup, then spread a thin layer of buttercream over the syrup with the angled metal spatula and put the cakes together to form a ball shape. Using the angled metal spatula, cover the cake with buttercream **(a)**, then chill in the refrigerator 2 hours until set. Repeat with the remaining cake halves to make two buttercream-covered ball cakes in total.

5 When the buttercream has set, dust the work surface with a little powdered sugar, then knead the red gum paste until it is soft and pliable. Roll out the kneaded gum paste until it is ¼in. thick, using marzipan spacers, if you like. Lift the rolled gum paste and gently drape it over the top of one of the cake balls. Using your hands, smooth the gum paste over the cake, covering it completely, but take care not to stretch or pull the gum paste. Gather the gum paste at the base of the cake **(b)**. Trim off the excess gum paste with the sharp knife, then flatten the base slightly **(c)**—this will allow the cake to stand unsupported. Smooth the gum paste again using the icing smoother. Decide which section of the cake will be the front, then concentrate on making that section look as smooth and neat as possible, hiding any creases in the gum paste at the back of the cake. Repeat with the remaining ball cake, and the orange gum paste. Decorate the ball cakes immediately.

(a)

(b)

(c)

CHRISTMAS DECORATIONS

For the Red Bauble Cake

MAKES 1 BAUBLE CAKE
½ piece of dry spaghetti
powdered sugar, for dusting
1oz. caramel-colored gum paste
    (see pages 160–1)
edible glue or cooled, boiled
    water
3¼in. ball cake, covered in red-
    colored gum paste
    (see page 92)
gold edible lustre dust
2 tbsp. red-colored soft-peak
    Royal Icing (see page 46)

YOU WILL NEED
parchment paper
small rolling pin
¼in. marzipan spacers
    (optional)
sharp knife
ruler
straight frill cutter (optional)
1⅓in. plain round circle cutter
    (optional)
small paintbrushes
pastry bag with a no. 2 plain
    tip attached

1 This recipe makes one cake but if you want to make more than one, simply scale up the amount of the listed ingredients. To make the loop for the top of the bauble, soak the piece of spaghetti in a mug of boiling water 10 minutes, or until it is soft and pliable. Bend the spaghetti into a loop (see picture on page 95), then transfer it to a piece of parchment paper to dry.

2 Dust the work surface with a little powdered sugar, then knead the caramel gum paste until it is soft and pliable. Roll out the gum paste until it is ¼in. thick, using marzipan spacers if you like, then cut a 6 x 1¼in. strip. Stamp a decorative border on the edge of the strip with the straight frill cutter or cut out a frill pattern with the sharp knife (see picture on page 95).

3 Roll the caramel gum paste trimmings into a ball, then reroll until it is ¼in. thick. Cut out a circle using the circle cutter. Alternatively, cut out a circle about 1⅓in. in diameter using the sharp knife. Turn the circle upside down, then brush the edges with a little edible glue. Attach the decorative border to the edge of the circle, creating a sunlike effect (see picture on page 95). Attach this to the top of the covered ball cake with a little more edible glue. Roll a pea-sized ball of caramel gum paste into a cylinder, then attach this to the center of the circle with edible glue. Push the bottom of the spaghetti loop into the cylinder and secure in place with edible glue. Leave the cake to dry overnight, uncovered, in a cool, dry place.

4 When the gum paste is completely dry, put a little gold edible lustre dust in a small bowl. Add water, a few drops at a time, and mix until a thick paint forms. Paint the caramel gum paste and the spaghetti loop with the lustre paint and leave to dry completely.

5 When the lustre paint has dried, spoon the royal icing into the pastry bag and pipe loops and curvy lines from the top of the bauble working downward (see picture on page 95). If you are not confident about piping loops and curves, pipe straight lines of various lengths down the side of the bauble. Embellish your design with dots of royal icing, if you like. (For hints on piping, see pages 157–9.) Leave the cake overnight, uncovered, in a cool, dry place to allow the icing to set.

**MAKES 1 ORANGE
    POMANDER CAKE**
3¼in ball cake, covered in
    orange-colored gum paste
    (see page 92)
powdered sugar, for dusting
1¾oz. red-colored flower paste
    (see pages 160–1)
edible glue or cooled, boiled
    water
¼ cup dark brown soft-peak
    Royal Icing (see page 46)

YOU WILL NEED
toothpick
small rolling pin
sharp knife
ruler
**design wheeler tool with stitch
    head**
small paintbrush
bow templates (see page 165)
tissue paper
**pastry bag with a no. 1.5 plain
    tip attached**

For the Orange Pomander Cake

1 This recipe makes one cake but if you want to make more than one, simply scale up the amount of the listed ingredients. Blunt the end of the toothpick slightly, then indent tiny holes all over the orange gum paste—this will take time, but care taken at this stage will produce a more realistic effect overall. Leave the cake to dry overnight, uncovered, in a cool, dry place.

2 Dust the work surface with a little powdered sugar and knead the red flower paste until it is smooth and elastic. Roll out the red flower paste very thinly, then cut into 4 strips, each about 4½ x ⅝in. Use the design wheeler tool to indent a "stitched" line along the edges of each strip. Arrange the strips over the ball to form a cross at the top of the cake, then secure them to the cake with a little edible glue.

3 Roll the red flower paste trimmings into a ball, then reroll quite thinly. Place the templates for the bow on top of the rolled flower paste and cut around them with the sharp knife, then use the design wheeler tool to indent a "stitched" line along the edges of each strip. Attach the tail pieces to the top of the cake, draping them down the side, then pinch them together slightly at the top. Secure the tail pieces in place with edible glue.

4 Take one of the loop pieces and brush one of the short ends with a little edible glue, then fold it in half to form a loop, pinching it in slightly at the join. Repeat with the remaining loop piece to make 2 loops. Stuff the hollow of each loop with a small piece of crumpled tissue paper—this will keep the flower paste in position while it dries. Place the loops at the top of the cake to form a bow, securing each one with edible glue. Mold the bow join over and around the spot where the bow loops meet, and secure with a little edible glue.

5 Spoon the royal icing into the pastry bag. To achieve the studded-clove effect along the edges of the ribbon, pipe a little cross, then immediately pipe a dot over the top to make a "clove." Repeat along the edges of each ribbon, starting at the top edges and working your way down to the base. (For hints on piping, see pages 157–9.) Leave the cake overnight, uncovered, in a cool, dry place to allow the decoration to set. Remove the tissue paper from the bow before serving.

Christmas Pudding Cake

MAKES 1 CAKE
2 x 6in. ball cake halves in your
  choice of sponge cake (see
  pages 56–7, 62–3 and 76–7)
1 recipe quantity Sugar Syrup
  (see page 119)
1 recipe quantity Vanilla
  Buttercream (see page 16)
powdered sugar, for dusting
2lb. 4oz. dark brown-colored
  gum paste (see pages 160–1)
5½oz. white gum paste
  (see pages 160–1)
edible glue or cooled, boiled
  water
⅛oz. black-colored gum paste
  (see pages 160–1)
½oz. red-colored gum paste
  (see pages 160–1)
1¾oz. dark green-colored gum
  paste (see pages 160–1)

YOU WILL NEED
long serrated knife
pastry brush
angled metal spatula
rolling pin
¼in. marzipan spacers
  (optional)
sharp knife
icing smoother
paintbrush
holly leaf template
  (see page 162)

1 Using the serrated knife, level the flat-side of the ball cake halves to ensure they will create a neat ball shape when held together, then slice each cake in half horizontally to form four layers. Lightly brush the cut sides of the cakes with sugar syrup. Stacking the layers back together, fill and cover the cake with buttercream using the angled metal spatula. (For hints on filling and covering ball cakes with buttercream, see page 92.) Chill in the refrigerator 2 hours until set.

2 When the buttercream has set, dust the work surface with a little powdered sugar, then knead the dark brown gum paste until it is soft and pliable. Roll out the kneaded gum paste until it is ¼in. thick, using marzipan spacers if you like. Lift the rolled gum paste and gently drape it over the top of the cake. Using your hands, smooth the gum paste over the cake, covering it completely, but take care not to stretch or pull the gum paste. Gather the gum paste at the base of the cake. Trim off the excess gum paste with the sharp knife, then flatten the base slightly—this will allow the cake to stand unsupported. Smooth the gum paste again using the icing smoother. (For hints on covering ball cakes in gum paste, see page 92.) Roll the trimmings into a ball and store in an airtight container so the gum paste does not dry out and crack.

3 For the brandy sauce, dust the work surface with a little more powdered sugar, then knead the white gum paste until it is soft and pliable. Roll out the kneaded gum paste into a circle about 4in. in diameter and about ¼in. thick, using marzipan spacers, if you like. Cut a wavy line around the edge using the sharp knife. Lightly brush the top of the cake with edible glue and place the wavy white gum paste over the top, pressing down gently to secure. Roll the trimmings into a ball and store in an airtight container so the gum paste does not dry out and crack.

4 For the nuts, roll the black gum paste into 15 tiny balls. For the candied citrus peel, knead a tiny amount of dark brown gum paste into ⅛oz. of the remaining white gum paste to form a small amount of light brown gum paste, then roll this into 6 tiny balls. For the dried fruit, roll ⅛oz. of the red gum paste into 9 tiny balls. Brush the nuts, peel and dried fruits with a little edible glue, then attach them around the side of the cake.

5 For the holly leaves, dust the work surface with a little more powdered sugar, then knead the dark green gum paste until it is soft and pliable. Roll out the kneaded gum paste quite thinly, then cut out 3 holly leaves using the template and indent veins onto each one with the sharp knife. Brush the back of the leaves with a little edible glue and attach them to the top of the cake, curling them slightly if you like. For the holly berries, roll the remaining red gum paste into 3 small balls. Brush the base of the berries with a little edible glue and attach them to the center of the leaves. Leave the cake overnight, uncovered, in a cool, dry place to allow the gum paste to dry.

Easter Hen Cookies

**MAKES 6 HEN AND
12 EGG COOKIES**
1 scant cup dark brown-colored
 soft-peak Royal Icing (see
 page 46)
6 hen cookies and 12 egg
 cookies made using ½ recipe
 quantity Cookie Dough of
 your choice (see pages 26–7),
 cut out with the hen and egg
 templates (see page 169)
¼ cup red-colored soft-peak
 Royal Icing (see page 46)
½ cup cream-colored soft-peak
 Royal Icing (see page 46)
1 tbsp. white soft-peak Royal
 Icing (see page 46)
1 tbsp. black-colored soft-peak
 Royal Icing (see page 46)

YOU WILL NEED
5 pastry bags, 3 with a
 no. 2 plain tip attached
3 plastic squeeze bottles

1 Spoon ¼ cup of the dark brown soft-peak royal icing into one of the pastry bags that has a no. 2 plain tip attached to it. Pipe a hen outline onto each of the hen cookies, avoiding the comb and wattle. (For hints on piping, see pages 157–9.) Spoon half of the red soft-peak royal icing into another pastry bag with a no. 2 plain tip attached and pipe outlines of the comb and wattle onto the hen cookies. Spoon 2 tablespoons of the cream soft-peak royal icing into the remaining pastry bag with a no. 2 plain tip attached and pipe a beak outline onto the hen cookies **(a)** and an egg outline onto the egg cookies. Leave the cookies at least 10 to 15 minutes, uncovered, in a cool, dry place to allow the icing to set.

2 Meanwhile, spoon the remaining dark brown, red and cream soft-peak royal icings into three separate bowls, then add enough water to each bowl to slacken the icings to flood consistency (see page 46). Pour the dark brown, red and cream flood icings into separate plastic squeeze bottles.

3 Decorating one cookie at a time, quickly and carefully flood the center of each hen cookie with the dark brown flood icing **(b)**, then gently squeeze small drops of cream flood icing onto the body of the hen to create a speckled effect **(c)**—if you do not do this immediately, the speckles will dry proud of the hen's body. Repeat with the remaining dark brown and cream flood icings and the remaining hen cookies until all the hens have speckled bodies. Flood the comb and wattle of the hen cookies with red flood icing, then flood the beaks with cream flood icing. Flood the center of the egg cookies with the remaining cream flood icing. Leave at least 1 hour, uncovered, in a cool, dry place to allow the icing to set.

4 When the icing has set, use the remaining dark brown soft-peak royal icing to pipe another hen outline around the edge of each cookie, then pipe the wing detail over the top of the hen's body. Spoon the white royal icing into one of the remaining pastry bags, then snip off the end if necessary. Pipe an eye onto the face of each hen and leave to dry 10 to 15 minutes. When the icing has dried, spoon the black royal icing into the remaining pastry bag, then snip off the tip if necessary. Pipe a tiny pupil on top of each eye. Leave overnight, uncovered, in a cool, dry place to allow the icing to set.

(a)

(b)

(c)

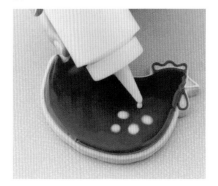

Mother's Day Cookies

MAKES 4 COOKIES
powdered sugar, for dusting
1¾oz. pink-colored gum paste
  (see pages 160–1)
edible glue or 2 tbsp. apricot
  jam, warmed
4 cookies made using ¼ recipe
  quantity Cookie Dough of your
  choice (see pages 26–7), cut
  out with the handbag, coin
  purse and shoe templates
  (see page 168)
¾oz. cream-colored gum paste
  (see pages 160–1)
¾oz. black-colored gum paste
  (see pages 160–1)
2¾oz. purple-colored gum paste
  (see pages 160–1)
silver edible lustre dust

YOU WILL NEED
small rolling pin
handbag, coin purse and shoe
  templates (see page 168)
sharp knife
ruler
small paintbrushes
small angled metal spatula
design wheeler tool with
  stitch head
double-ended ball tool
straight frill cutter (optional)
modeling pad or clean, dry
  folded tea towel

For the Pink Handbag

1 Dust the work surface with a little powdered sugar, then knead the pink gum paste until it is soft and pliable. Roll out the kneaded gum paste quite thinly and cut out a handbag, using the template. Using the ruler to help you, cut away the top of the handbag and trim the sides to form a rectangle. The width of the rectangle should be slightly smaller than the width of the cookie. Roll the trimmings into a ball and store in an airtight container so the gum paste does not dry out and crack.

2 Brush the underside of the pink rectangle with a little edible glue, then place it onto the handbag cookie using the angled metal spatula and taking care not to stretch it. To achieve the "quilted" effect, use the design wheeler tool to indent "stitched" diagonal lines across the gum paste **(a)**.

3 For the cream panel, roll out the cream gum paste quite thinly and cut a 4 x ½in. panel. Make two small indentations on either end of the panel with the large head of the ball tool **(a)**. Attach the panel to the cookie with edible glue so that it is flush with the pink gum paste. Trim as necessary.

4 For the handle, roll a large pea-sized ball of black gum paste. Split the ball in half and roll each one into a thin sausage about 6in. long. Twist the two together, then gently roll them on the work surface **(b)** to form one long handle cord. Trim the ends to neaten. Using the indentations made by the ball tool as a guide, attach the handle to the panel and to the cookie with edible glue.

5 For the tassels, roll 2 tiny balls of black gum paste and 2 even smaller balls of cream gum paste. Flatten all of the balls slightly. Using a little edible glue, attach the cream balls to the black balls and set aside. Roll 2 small balls of black gum paste and mold them into tear-drop shapes. Flatten them slightly, then make 3 or 4 cuts for the tassels, using the sharp knife **(c)**. Using edible glue, attach the tassels to the ends of the handle, then attach the black and cream balls to the top of the tassels (see picture on page 103).

(a)

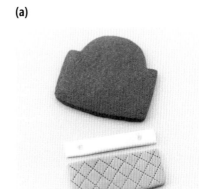

(b)

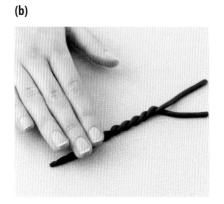

(c)

(d)

For the Pink Stiletto-Heeled Shoe

1 Dust the work surface with powdered sugar and roll out the remaining pink, black and cream gum pastes quite thinly. Using the template, cut out one shoe in each color.

2 Cut out the central section of the pink shoe; the toe and heel of the cream shoe; and the stiletto heel, sole and toe detail of the black shoe. For the heel tip, score a line in the black gum paste at the base of the stiletto heel with the sharp knife. Roll the trimmings into balls and store in an airtight container so the gum paste does not dry out and crack.

3 To achieve the "quilted" effect on the central section, use the design wheeler tool to indent "stitched" diagonal lines across the pink gum paste. Using the angled metal spatula, arrange the various gum paste sections **(d)** onto the stiletto-heeled shoe cookie, trimming as necessary to achieve a neat finish. Brush the surface of the cookie with edible glue, then secure each gum-paste section in place, taking care not to stretch or pull them.

For the Purple Coin Purse

1 Dust the work surface with powdered sugar, then knead 1oz. of the purple gum paste until it is soft and pliable. For the frills, roll out the kneaded paste quite thinly, then cut into 4 strips, each about 4 x ¾in. Stamp out a frill on the edge of the strips with the straight frill cutter **(e)** or cut out a frill pattern with the sharp knife. Place the strips on the modeling pad, then gently roll the large head of the ball tool over the frill to soften the edges **(f)**.

2 Using edible glue to secure all the layers, attach one frill to the bottom of the coin-purse cookie, then overlap the remaining frills until you have covered the entire cookie **(g)**. Do not cover the kiss-lock closure in purple gum paste. Trim the frills as necessary.

(e)

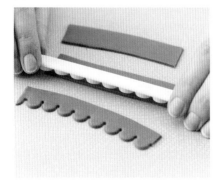

(f)

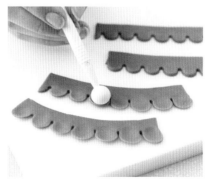

(g)

3 For the kiss-lock closure, roll a pea-sized quantity of the cream gum paste into a little sausage and attach it at the top of the cookie with edible glue, trimming the edges as necessary. Roll 2 tiny balls of cream gum paste and attach them to the center of the sausage to form a clasp. When the gum paste is completely dry, put a little silver edible lustre dust in a small bowl. Add water, a few drops at a time, and mix until a thick paint forms. Paint the kiss-lock closure with the lustre paint and leave to dry completely. Cover the unused paint with plastic wrap and set aside until needed.

For the Purple Pump Shoe

1 Dust the work surface with powdered sugar, then knead the remaining purple gum paste until it is soft and pliable. Roll out the kneaded paste quite thinly and cut out a pump shoe, using the template. Cut away a little gum paste at the top of the shoe to create a foot hole **(h)**. Using the gum-paste shoe as a guide, brush the pump-shoe cookie with edible glue. Using the angled metal spatula, place the gum-paste shoe onto the cookie, taking care not to stretch or pull it **(i)**, then gently smooth it over the cookie with your fingers.

2 Use the design wheeler tool to indent "stitched" seams onto the shoe, then score a line for the heel tip at the bottom of the heel using the back of the sharp knife.

3 To make the rose, reroll the purple gum-paste trimmings quite thinly and cut a 4 x ½in. strip. Stamp a frill onto the edge of the strip with the straight frill cutter or cut out a frill pattern with the sharp knife. Gently roll up the strip to form a rose **(j)**. Pinch the gum paste together at the bottom of the rose, then cut off the excess gum paste to form a flat base and attach the rose to the shoe with a little edible glue. Roll a tiny ball of cream gum paste and attach it to the center of the rose with a little edible glue. When the gum paste is completely dry, paint the center of the rose with the lustre paint and leave to dry completely.

(h)   **(i)**   **(j)**

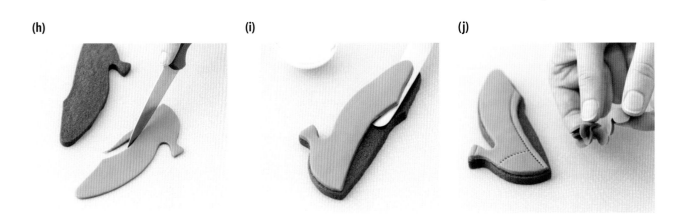

Birthday Butterfly Mini Domes

MAKES 4 CAKES
powdered sugar, for dusting
7oz. pale yellow-colored gum
   paste (see pages 160–1)
7oz. pale blue-colored gum
   paste (see pages 160–1)
4 prepared Sponge Cakes or
   Marble Dome Mini Cakes
   (see page 128)
1¾oz. yellow-colored modeling
   paste (see pages 160–1)
1¾oz. dark blue-colored
   modeling paste
   (see pages 160–1)
2 tbsp. black-colored stiff-peak
   Royal Icing (see page 46)

YOU WILL NEED
small rolling pin
¼in. marzipan spacers
   (optional)
sharp knife
ruler
butterfly templates
   (see page 169)
baking sheet lined with
   parchment paper, plus extra
   parchment paper for lining the
   "troughs"
pastry bag with a no. 2 plain tip
   attached
8 x 11in. sheet of thin cardboard

HINTS
For tips on baking ball cake
halves, see page 92.

You will need to cover the
cakes and make the butterfly
wings at least a day before they
are needed. (For more hints on
assembling sugarcraft butterflies,
see page 116.)

1 Dust the work surface with a little powdered sugar, then knead the pale yellow gum paste until it is soft and pliable. Roll out the kneaded gum paste until it is ¼in. thick, using marzipan spacers, if you like. Cut out 2 squares, each measuring 5 x 5in. Repeat with the pale blue gum paste to make four squares of gum paste in total. Following the instructions on page 153, use one square of gum paste to cover each cake, trimming as necessary. Leave the cakes overnight, uncovered, in a cool, dry place to allow the gum paste to dry.

2 To make the butterflies, dust the work surface with more powdered sugar, then knead the yellow modeling paste until it is soft and pliable. Roll out the kneaded modeling paste quite thinly and cut out 2 large butterflies and 2 small butterflies, using the templates. Dust the work surface with a little more powdered sugar and repeat with the dark blue modeling paste to make eight butterflies in total. Cut each butterfly in half vertically and transfer the wings to the prepared baking sheet.

3 Spoon the royal icing into the pastry bag and pipe the outline of the wings onto each butterfly. (For hints on piping, see pages 157–9.) Roll up the pastry bag and store in an airtight container until needed. Leave the outlined butterfly wings to dry, overnight, uncovered, in a cool, dry place.

4 When the gum paste and butterfly wings have dried, crease the sheet of cardboard along the long edge into 3 concertina folds to make a deep v-shaped "trough"—this will help you to assemble the butterflies and allow the wings to dry at an angle (see picture, page 116). Cut out a 24 x 4in. strip of parchment paper, then fold it in half along the long edge and use it to line the center of the "trough." To assemble the large butterflies, pipe a 1¼in. line of royal icing along the bottom crease of the "trough." Take one set of large butterfly wings and gently press the cut side of each one into the icing to create a butterfly. Starting at the tail end, pipe a second line of royal icing along the center of the butterfly for the body and finish with a large dot of icing for the head (see picture). Repeat with the remaining large butterflies. To assemble the small butterflies, pipe ⅝in. lines of royal icing along the bottom crease and repeat as above. Roll up the pastry bag and store in an airtight container until needed. Leave the butterflies to dry in the "trough" at least 2 hours.

5 When the assembled butterflies are stable and completely dry, carefully attach one large butterfly and one small one to the top of each cake, securing them with a dot of royal icing. Leave the cakes at least 10 to 15 minutes, uncovered, in a cool, dry place to allow the icing to set.

Santa's Sleigh Cake

MAKES 1 CAKE
¼ cup apricot jam, warmed
7in. round Fruit Cake
   (see pages 108–9)
powdered sugar, for dusting
1lb. 10oz. marzipan
1lb. 11oz. white gum paste
   (see pages 160–1)
3½oz. red-colored modeling
   paste (see pages 160–1)
¼oz. each of green-, dark pink-,
   lilac-,orange- and pale yellow-
   colored gum pastes or brightly
   colored gum pastes of your
   choice (see pages 160–1)
¼ cup white soft-peak Royal
   Icing (see page 46)

YOU WILL NEED
pastry brush
7in. round cake board
small rolling pin
¼in. marzipan spacers
   (optional)
sleigh templates (see page 169)
sharp knife
small angled metal spatula
baking sheet lined with
   parchment paper
ruler
pastry bag with a no. 1.5 plain
   tip attached
24in. piece red satin ribbon,
   1⅓in. wide

HINT
You will need to cover the cake in
marzipan the day before you want
to cover it with gum paste.

1 Brush the top of the cake board with a little jam, then attach the cake to the board, upside down, to give the cake a flat top. Dust the work surface with a little powdered sugar, then knead the marzipan until it is soft, but take care not to overknead it. Fill any gaps around the base of the cake with a little of the kneaded marzipan. Following the instructions on page 153, cover the cake with the remaining kneaded marzipan, followed the next day by 1lb. 10oz. of kneaded white gum paste. Leave the gum paste-covered cake overnight, uncovered, in a cool, dry place to allow the gum paste to dry.

2 Dust the work surface with a little powdered sugar, then knead the red modeling paste until it is soft and pliable. Roll out the kneaded modeling paste until it is ¼in. thick, using marzipan spacers if you like. Place the templates for the front, back and side panels of the sleigh on the rolled modeling paste and cut around them with the sharp knife. You will need 1 front panel, 1 back panel and 2 side panels. Smooth the edges of each panel with your fingers. Using the angled metal spatula, transfer the panels to the prepared baking sheet, taking care not to stretch or pull the modeling paste.

3 To make the sleigh's runners, dust the work surface with a little more powdered sugar, then knead the remaining white gum paste until it is soft and pliable. Divide the gum paste into two balls, then roll each one into a long, thin sausage about 5in. long. Flatten the sausages slightly, then curl the ends of each one back on itself (see picture). For the presents, knead each of the brightly colored gum pastes until soft and pliable. Mold the kneaded gum pastes into 10 different shapes, such as cubes, rectangles and spheres. Transfer the runners and presents to the prepared baking sheet. Leave the sleigh panels, runners and presents to dry overnight, uncovered, in a cool, dry place.

4 When the gum paste and decorations have dried, spoon the royal icing into the pastry bag. Pipe the ribbon details onto each present, then pipe the swirl design along the top of the side panels of the sleigh (see picture). (For hints on piping, see pages 157–9.) Leave the icing to set 10 to 15 minutes. Meanwhile, wrap the ribbon around the bottom of the cake, securing the join at the back with a little royal icing and trimming as necessary. Pipe small dots of royal icing just above the top of the ribbon, evenly spacing them around the cake (see picture).

5 To assemble the sleigh, pipe a line of royal icing along the inside edges of the front and back sleigh panels, then gently press the side panels into position. Hold the sleigh in place a few seconds while the icing sets, then support the panels with drinking glasses and leave to dry at least 1 hour, uncovered, in a cool, dry place. Roll up the pastry bag and store in an airtight container until needed. When the sleigh is stable, carefully place it in the center of the cake, securing it with a little royal icing. Attach the runners to the cake along the base of the sleigh, then place the presents inside, securing each one with royal icing. Leave to set, uncovered, in a cool, dry place, before serving.

Fruit Cake

The table opposite shows you the quantity of ingredients and baking times required for different cake sizes and styles. It also offers advice on serving portions. Simply select your size and style and follow the method below.

dates
prunes
dried apricots
golden raisins
raisins
currants
candied cherries
orange zest
lemon zest
orange juice
lemon juice
brandy
salted butter
dark brown sugar
molasses
eggs
all-purpose flour
baking powder
ground cinnamon
ground ginger
ground nutmeg
ground mixed spice
chopped candied ginger
vanilla extract

YOU WILL NEED
cake pan lined with parchment
  paper (for hints on lining cake
  pans, see page 149)

HINT
The cake can be kept for up to
6 weeks to mature. Wrap it in a
double layer of parchment paper
and then in a layer of aluminum
foil. Store at room temperature
in a cool, dry place.

1 Snip the dates, prunes and apricots into thirds with kitchen scissors, then transfer to a large mixing bowl. Add the golden raisins, raisins, currants, candied cherries, orange and lemon zests and juices and brandy and mix well. Leave to steep, covered, 6 hours or overnight at room temperature.

2 At the end of the steeping time, preheat the oven to 275°F. Put the butter and sugar in a saucepan over low heat. Cook, stirring frequently, until the sugar has melted. Pour the mixture into a large mixing bowl, then add the molasses and eggs and mix well. Sift the flour, baking powder and spices into the bowl and fold in, using a metal spoon. Add the steeped fruits and their juices, then add the candied ginger and vanilla extract and mix until well combined.

3 Spoon the batter into the prepared cake pan, leveling the surface with the back of a metal spoon. Bake for the recommended time or until a skewer inserted into the center comes out clean. Oven temperatures can vary, so check on the cake about 5 minutes before the end of the recommended baking time.

4 Remove the cake from the oven and leave in the pan to cool completely. (For hints on covering the cake with marzipan and gum paste, see page 153.)

Use this fruit cake recipe for the following recipes throughout this book:

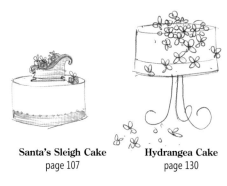

Santa's Sleigh Cake
page 107

Hydrangea Cake
page 130

	4in. round or square cake	5in. round or square cake	6in. round or square cake	7in. round or square cake	8in. round, square or heart cake	9in. round or square cake
dates	3 tbsp.	scant ¼ cup	¼ cup	heaped ⅓ cup	scant ½ cup	⅔ cup
prunes	2 tbsp.	3 tbsp.	scant ¼ cup	scant ⅓ cup	heaped ⅓ cup	heaped ½ cup
dried apricots	3½ tbsp.	scant ¼ cup	¼ cup	heaped ⅓ cup	½ cup	⅔ cup
golden raisins	½ cup	scant ⅔ cup	scant 1 cup	scant 1½ cups	scant 2 cups	2½ cups
raisins	½ cup	scant ⅔ cup	scant 1 cup	scant 1½ cups	scant 2 cups	2½ cups
currants	½ cup	⅔ cup	1 cup	scant 1½ cups	2 cups	2⅔ cups
candied cherries	¼ cup	⅓ cup	½ cup	⅔ cup	¾ cup	1¼ cups
orange zest	½ orange	1 orange	1 orange	1½ oranges	2 oranges	2½ oranges
lemon zest	½ lemon	1 lemon	1 lemon	1½ lemons	2 lemons	2½ lemons
orange juice	1 tbsp.	1 tbsp.	1 tbsp.	2 tbsp.	2 tbsp.	2–3 tbsp.
lemon juice	1 tbsp.	1 tbsp.	2 tbsp.	2 tbsp.	2 tbsp.	2–3 tbsp.
brandy	3 tbsp.	generous ¼ cup	generous ⅓ cup	scant ⅔ cup	scant 1 cup	generous 1 cup
salted butter	¼ cup (½ stick)	⅓ cup (⅔ stick)	heaped ½ cup (1 stick)	scant 1 cup (2 sticks)	1¼ cups (2½ sticks)	1½ cups (3 sticks)
dark brown sugar	heaped ⅓ cup	scant ½ cup	heaped ⅔ cup	heaped 1 cup	heaped 1⅓ cups	scant 2 cups
molasses	1½ tsp.	1½ tsp.	1 tbsp.	1 tbsp.	1 tbsp.	2 tbsp.
eggs	2 medium	2 medium	3 medium	4 medium	5 large	7 medium
all-purpose flour	½ cup	scant ⅔ cup	scant 1 cup	scant 1½ cups	scant 2 cups	heaped 2½ cups
baking powder	¼ tsp.	¼ tsp.	¼ tsp.	½ tsp.	½ tsp.	¾ tsp.
ground cinnamon	¼ tsp.	¼ tsp.	¾ tsp.	1¼ tsp.	1½ tsp.	2 tsp.
ground ginger	¼ tsp.	¼ tsp.	¾ tsp.	1¼ tsp.	1½ tsp.	2 tsp.
ground nutmeg	¼ tsp.	¼ tsp.	¾ tsp.	1¼ tsp.	1½ tsp.	2 tsp.
ground mixed spice	¼ tsp.	¼ tsp.	¾ tsp.	1¼ tsp.	1½ tsp.	2 tsp.
chopped candied ginger	1 tbsp.	1½ tbsp.	2 tbsp.	2½ tbsp.	3 tbsp.	scant ¼ cup
vanilla extract	¼ tsp.	¼ tsp.	¼ tsp.	½ tsp.	½ tsp.	¾ tsp.
baking time	1¼ hours	1½ hours	2 hours	2¼ hours	2½ hours	2¾ hours
serves	10	12	15–20	20–30	30–40	40–50

Baby Shower Cupcakes

MAKES 6 CUPCAKES
powdered sugar, for dusting
5½oz. blue-colored modeling
   paste (see pages 160–1)
2¼oz. cream-colored gum paste
   (see pages 160–1)
¼oz. black-colored gum paste
   (see pages 160–1)
5½oz. pink-colored modeling
   paste (see page 160–1)
edible glue or cooled, boiled
   water
2 pieces of dry spaghetti,
   each one snapped into 3 small
   pieces (optional)
½ recipe quantity Vanilla
   Frosting (see page 118)
6 Cupcakes in a flavor of your
   choice (see page 129)

YOU WILL NEED
ruler
small paintbrush
double-ended ball tool
design wheeler tool with
   stitch head
sharp knife
pastry bag with a ¾in. closed-
   star tip attached
6 cupcake wrappers

HINT
You will need to make the bears
and rabbits the day before they
are needed.

1 This recipe makes six cupcakes but if you only want to make one, simply decide whether you would like to make a bear or a rabbit and scale down the listed ingredients. Dust the work surface with powdered sugar, then knead all of the modeling and gum pastes until they are soft and pliable. Store the kneaded pastes in an airtight container until needed so they do not dry out and crack.

2 To make a teddy bear, dust the work surface with a little more powdered sugar. For the bear's body, roll ¾oz. of the blue modeling paste into a tear-drop shape. For the arms and legs, roll ¼oz. of the blue modeling paste into 4 balls. Roll each of the balls into tapered sausages about 1½in. long, then slightly flatten the thicker ends to form paws. For the paw pads, roll 4 small pea-sized balls of cream gum paste and attach them to the paws with edible glue, flattening them slightly as you do so. Using the picture as a guide, mold the legs and arms around the body, then attach with edible glue.

3 To make the head, roll ¼oz. of the blue modeling paste into a ball. For the ears, roll 2 pea-sized balls of blue modeling paste and indent the center of each one with the small head of the ball tool. While the modeling paste is still soft, use the wheeler tool to indent "stitched" lines along the bear's body, arms, legs and head. Attach the head to the body using edible glue. Insert a piece of dry spaghetti into the bear's body to support the head and hold it in place, if necessary.

4 To make the muzzle, roll a pea-sized ball of cream-colored gum paste, then flatten it into an oval. Attach the ears and muzzle to the head with a little edible glue. For the nose, roll a small ball of blue modeling paste. Attach the nose to the muzzle with edible glue, flattening it slightly as you do so, then indent a line coming down from the nose with the sharp knife (see picture). For the eyes, roll 2 tiny balls of black gum paste and attach with edible glue. Repeat steps 2–4 to make three bears.

5 To make a rabbit, repeat steps 2–4 above using pink modeling paste instead of blue. To make rabbit ears instead of bear ears, roll 2 pea-sized balls of pink modeling paste and 2 tiny balls of cream-colored gum paste and mold each one into a tear-drop shape. Using edible glue, attach the cream tear drops to the center of the pink tear drops. Attach the ears to the head with a little edible glue. Repeat to make three rabbits in total.

6 Leave the bears and rabbits to dry overnight, uncovered in a cool dry place. When the bears and rabbits have dried, spoon the frosting into the pastry bag and pipe a high swirl (see page 157) onto each cupcake. (For hints on piping, see pages 157–9.) Put each cupcake in a cupcake wrapper, then place a bear or rabbit on top of each one, gently pressing them into the center of the frosting swirl to hold them in place.

CHAPTER FOUR

With a little time and patience it's easy to make a range
of stunning treats. Add the "Wow!" factor to any party with
a Gift-Wrapped Cake. The Butterfly Fancies will be the talk
of the tea party, and your friends and family will be absolutely
amazed when they see the Teapot Cake. Everything looks too
good to eat, but trust me, that won't stop anyone.

DECORATE
TO
IMPRESS

Ivory Corsage Wedding Cake

MAKES 1 CAKE
2 x 4in. round Chocolate Sponge Cakes (see pages 62–3)
2 x 8in. round Chocolate Sponge Cakes (see pages 62–3)
2 recipe quantities Chocolate Ganache (see page 16)
6in. round Rich Chocolate Cake (see pages 56–7)
powdered sugar, for dusting
4lb. 8oz. ivory-colored gum paste (see pages 160–1)
7oz. ivory modeling paste (see pages 160–1)
edible glue or cooled, boiled water
¼ cup ivory-colored stiff-peak Royal Icing (see page 46)

YOU WILL NEED
4in. round cake board
8in. round cake board
6in. round cake board
small rolling pin
small and large corsage templates (see page 165)
sharp knife
modeling pad or a clean, dry folded tea towel
double-ended ball tool
indented foam pad or a piece of crinkled aluminum foil
small paintbrush
pastry bag with a no. 2 plain tip attached
plastic dowel rods
5ft. ivory satin ribbon, ⅝in. wide
small and large leaf templates (see page 165)

HINT
You will need to make the corsages at least a day before they are needed. (For hints on making corsages, see page 53).

1 Following the instructions on page 150 and using the cake boards as firm bases, layer the 4in. chocolate sponge cakes and the 8in. chocolate sponge cakes, then fill with chocolate ganache to make one tall 4in. cake and one tall 8in. cake. Following the instructions on page 152, cover each tier of the cake with the remaining ganache. Chill in the refrigerator at least 2 hours. When the ganache has set, dust the work surface with a little powdered sugar, then knead 1lb. 14oz. of the ivory gum paste until it is soft and pliable. Following the instructions on page 153, cover the 8in. cake with the kneaded gum paste. Repeat as above using 1lb. 6oz. of gum paste to cover the 6in. cake and 15oz. to cover the 4in. cake.

2 To make a corsage, dust the work surface with powdered sugar and knead 1oz. of the ivory modeling paste until it is soft and pliable. For the center of the corsage, roll a blueberry-sized ball of modeling paste. Roll out the remaining kneaded paste quite thinly. Place the templates for the small and large flowers onto the rolled modeling paste and cut around them with the sharp knife. You will need 1 small flower and 2 large flowers. Place the flowers on the modeling pad, then gently roll the large head of the ball tool over each petal to soften the edges. Place one of the large flowers on the indented foam pad. Brush a little edible glue in the center of the large flower, then set the other large flower on the top. Attach the central ball to the center of the small flower, wrapping the petals of the flower around the ball, then attach it to the center of the corsage: to achieve a closed-bud effect, secure the petals tightly to the ball with a little edible glue; to achieve an opened-bud effect, wrap the petals around the ball attaching them with a little edible glue at the base only. Making one corsage at a time, repeat with 4¼oz. of the ivory modeling paste to make four corsages in total. Leave the cakes and corsages to dry overnight, uncovered, in a cool, dry place.

3 When the gum paste and corsages have dried, spoon the royal icing into the pastry bag. Following the instructions on page 156, stack the cakes on top of each other with plastic dowel rods. Wrap the ribbon around the bottom of each tier, securing the join at the back with a little royal icing and trimming as necessary. Position the corsages over the cake tiers and secure them in place with a little royal icing. Dust the work surface with a little powdered sugar, then knead the remaining ivory modeling paste until it is soft and pliable. Roll out the kneaded paste quite thinly. Assessing how many extra petals you will need to fill the gaps between the corsages and the cake, cut around the large flower template as many times as is necessary, then cut each flower into 5 petals. Soften the edges of the petals as above in step 2. While the petals are still soft, attach them to the cake behind the corsage flowers to make four full corsages in total, securing each one in place with a little royal icing. Starting from the corsages, pipe 3 or 4 curvy lines onto the cake. Roll the modeling paste trimmings into a ball, then reroll quite thinly and cut out 8 small leaves and 8 large leaves using the templates. Soften each leaf as above in step 2, then pinch together the base of each one to form an inward curve. Attach the leaves to the cake along the curvy piped lines, securing each one with a little royal icing. Leave the cake overnight, uncovered, in a cool, dry place to allow the icing to set.

Butterfly Fancies

MAKES 16 FANCIES
7in. square Vanilla Sponge Cake
   (see pages 62–3), cooled
1 recipe quantity Vanilla Sugar
   Syrup (see page 119)
½ recipe quantity Vanilla
   Buttercream (see page 16)
2 heaped tbsp. seedless
   raspberry jam
powdered sugar, for dusting
6oz. marzipan
2 tbsp. apricot jam
4¾ cups dry fondant
yellow food coloring paste
turquoise food coloring paste
green food coloring paste
lilac food coloring paste
¼ cup white stiff-peak
   Royal Icing (see page 46)

YOU WILL NEED
16 foil baking cups
butterfly templates
   (see page 168)
8 x 11in. sheet of paper
baking sheet
parchment paper
pastry bag with a no. 2 plain
   tip attached
4 x 8 x 11in. sheets of thin
   cardboard
ruler
small angled metal spatula

1 Following steps 1–4 on page 18, make 16 unfrosted fancies. Following the instructions on page 151, cover one-quarter of the fancies in pale yellow, turquoise, green and lilac (not shown) fondant, then wrap in baking cups. Mix one batch of dry fondant at a time according to the package instructions. Leave the fancies to dry until the fondant has set, then cover and store at room temperature until needed.

2 Trace 16 pairs of butterfly wings onto the sheet of paper. Place the sheet of paper on the baking sheet and lay a sheet of parchment paper over the top. To allow for breakages, trace 20 pairs of wings onto the sheet of paper. Use masking tape or drinking glasses to hold the parchment paper in place—your piping may smudge if the parchment paper moves. Spoon the royal icing into the pastry bag. Piping one wing at a time, pipe over the outline of the wing, then pipe a random "lacework" pattern to completely cover the center of the wing **(a)**. (For hints on piping, see pages 157–9.) Repeat until you have at least 32 piped wings in total. Leave to dry overnight, uncovered, in a cool, dry place. Roll up the pastry bag and store in an airtight container until needed.

3 When the wings have dried, crease each sheet of cardboard along the long edge into 3 concertina folds to make four v-shaped "troughs"—this will help you to assemble the butterflies and allow the wings to dry at an angle. Cut out 4 strips of parchment paper, each about 24 x 4in., then fold them in half along the long edge and use them to line the center of the "troughs." To assemble a butterfly, pipe a 1¼in. line of royal icing along the bottom crease of one of the "troughs." Carefully lift a pair of wings away from the parchment paper with the angled metal spatula, then gently press each one into the icing to create a butterfly **(b)**. Starting at the tail end, pipe a second line of icing along the center of the butterfly for the body and finish with a large dot of icing for the head **(c)**. Repeat with the remaining sets of butterfly wings to make 16 butterflies in total. Leave the butterflies to dry in the "troughs" at least 2 hours. Roll up the pastry bag and store in an airtight container until needed. When the butterflies are stable and completely dry, carefully attach them to the top of the fondant fancies, securing each one with a little royal icing. Leave the fancies at least 10 to 15 minutes, uncovered, in a cool, dry place to allow the icing to set.

(a)

(b)

(c)

Basic Frosting

Frostings are piped onto cupcakes in decorative swirls to heighten their visual appeal and flavor. They have a much higher ratio of powdered sugar to butter than buttercream and as a result, frosted swirls "air dry" on the outside but stay soft on the inside. Plain and vanilla frostings can be colored with food coloring pastes. To color frosting, simply add a small amount of food coloring paste to the mixture, using the end of a toothpick, and mix until combined. Repeat until the desired color is achieved. (For hints on piping frosting swirls, see page 157.)

MAKES 12OZ.
2 cups powdered sugar
scant ½ cup (¾ stick) salted
  butter, softened
1 tbsp. milk
food coloring pastes (optional)

YOU WILL NEED
electric mixer
toothpick (optional)

For basic frosting, sift the powdered sugar into a mixing bowl. Add the butter and beat with the electric mixer until combined. With the mixer running, gradually add the milk. When all the milk is incorporated, beat 5 minutes until light and fluffy.

Variations

Chocolate Frosting: use 2½ cups powdered sugar and scant ½ cup unsweetened cocoa. Sift into the bowl together and beat with the butter as above. Use 3 tbsp. milk and add to the mixture as above.
Citrus Frosting: beat in the finely grated zest of 1 small lemon or 1 small orange along with the powdered sugar and butter.
Coffee Frosting: beat in ½ tsp. coffee extract with the powdered sugar and butter.
Vanilla Frosting: beat in ½ tsp. vanilla extract with the powdered sugar and butter.

CREAM CHEESE FROSTING

MAKES 1LB. 1OZ.
2½ cups powdered sugar
3½ tbsp. salted butter, softened
½ cup chilled cream cheese

YOU WILL NEED
electric mixer

Sift the powdered sugar into a mixing bowl. Add the butter and beat with the electric mixer until combined. Add all of the cream cheese, then beat about 5 minutes until light and fluffy. Take care not to overmix or the frosting will become too runny.

Use these frosting recipes for the following recipes throughout this book:

**Chocolate Swirl
Mini Cupcakes**
page 15

**Rose Swirl
Cupcakes**
page 22

**Rose Bouquet
Cupcakes**
page 67

**Chocolate Heart
Cake Pops**
page 68

**Baby Shower
Cupcakes**
page 110

Flower Cake Pops
page 132

Sugar Syrups

Lightly brushing sponge cakes with a little sugar syrup will keep them moist and also adds extra flavor. Take care not to use too much because it can make cakes overly sweet. Use it with any of the recipes listed below. To keep your cakes and cupcakes tasting as delicious as they look, I highly recommend brushing a little sugar syrup over any sponge cake you plan to cover and decorate over a 3–4 day period.

MAKES 1 RECIPE QUANTITY
½ cup superfine sugar

Put the sugar and scant ½ cup water in a saucepan and bring to a boil, without stirring. Leave to cool a little, then flavor, if you like (see below). Any leftover syrup can be kept in a sealed container in the refrigerator 2 weeks.

Flavors

Citrus: replace the water with scant ½ cup freshly squeezed orange or lemon juice.
Coffee: add 1 tbsp. coffee extract with the water.
Coffee Liqueur: add 1 tbsp. each of coffee extract and Amaretto or Tia Maria with the water.
Lemon Liqueur: replace the water with scant ½ cup freshly squeezed lemon juice and add 1 tbsp. Grand Marnier or limoncello.
Vanilla: add 1½ tsp. vanilla extract with the water.

Use this sugar syrup recipe for the following recipes throughout this book:

Fresh Flower Fondant Fancies
page 18

Mini Ghost Cakes
page 91

Festive Ball Cakes
page 92

Christmas Pudding Cake
page 97

Butterfly Fancies
page 116

Teapot Cake
page 122

Magnificent Mini Cakes

MAKES 4 MINI CAKES
powdered sugar, for dusting
1lb. 5oz. white gum paste
   (see pages 160–1)
4 prepared Sponge or Marble
   Round Mini Cakes
   (see page 128)
4¼oz. white flower paste
   (see pages 160–1)
¼ cup white soft-peak Royal
   Icing (see page 46)
¼ cup pale green-colored soft-
   peak Royal Icing (see page 46)

YOU WILL NEED
small rolling pin
¼in. marzipan spacers
   (optional)
sharp knife
ruler
swirly design (see page 169)
parchment paper
straight pins
scriber or sharp needle
2 pastry bags, each with
   no. 2 plain tips attached

HINT
Always leave the gum-paste
covered cakes to dry overnight
before you start scribing them.
This makes it far less likely that
you will accidently indent the
gum paste when decorating.

1 Dust the work surface with a little powdered sugar, then knead the white gum paste until it is soft and pliable. Roll out the kneaded gum paste until it is ¼in. thick, using marzipan spacers, if you like. Cut out 4 squares, each measuring 5¼ x 5¼in. Following the instructions on page 153, use one square of gum paste to cover each cake.

2 Knead 1oz. of the flower paste until it is smooth and elastic. Following steps 1–3 on page 126, make a small open rose. Repeat with the remaining flower paste to make four small roses in total. Leave the cakes and the roses overnight, uncovered, in a cool, dry place to allow the gum and flower pastes to dry.

3 When the pastes have dried, trace the swirly design onto a sheet of parchment paper 4 times, then closely cut around the outline of each swirl to make 4 scribing guides. Cut out 4 circles of parchment paper that are larger than the bottom of each cake. Carefully place the cakes on top of the parchment circles—this will make the cakes easier to turn when decorating.

4 Using the picture as a guide, position one of the scribing guides over the cake. Hold the guide in place with a couple of pins, pushing them through the top and bottom points of the swirl design—if the guide moves during scribing, the swirly design will be messy and hard to pipe over. Lightly prick the outline of the swirly design onto the cake with the scriber. (For hints on scribing, see page 83.) Scribe another 3 swirly designs onto the cake, evenly spacing the designs around the side. Repeat with the remaining cakes, using a new scribing guide for each one.

5 Spoon the white and pale green soft-peak royal icings into the pastry bags. Using the indentations made by the scriber as a guide, pipe a line of white soft-peak royal icing from the top of the cake to the center of the swirly design, then carefully pipe over the details of the swirl. (For hints on piping, see pages 157–9.) Repeat until all the swirly designs have been piped over.

6 Spacing the lines evenly between the piped swirls, pipe 4 vertical lines of white soft-peak royal icing down the side of each cake—starting from the top and finishing with a small dot of icing at the base. Repeat with the pale green soft-peak royal icing, piping 2 vertical lines of green icing down each side of the vertical white lines. Pipe a small dot of pale green soft-peak royal icing in the center of each swirly design. Leave the cakes 1 hour, uncovered, in a cool, dry place to allow the icing to set. Roll up the pastry bags and store in an airtight container until needed.

7 When the icing has dried, attach a flower paste rose to the top of each cake, securing it in place with a dot of white soft-peak royal icing.

Teapot Cake

MAKES 1 CAKE
2 x 6in. Mocha Sponge Cake ball
cake halves (see pages 62–3)
1 recipe quantity Vanilla
Buttercream (see page 16)
1 recipe quantity Sugar Syrup
(see page 119)
powdered sugar, for dusting
11½oz. ivory-colored or
white modeling paste
(see pages 160–1)
3lb. ivory-colored or white gum
paste (see pages 160–1)
white soft-peak Royal Icing
(see page 46)
¾oz. dark blue-colored gum
paste (see pages 160–1)
1 tbsp. cocoa butter beans
dark blue, light blue, white and
green edible food dusts

YOU WILL NEED
serrated knives
sharp knife
pastry brush
rolling pins
¼in. marzipan spacers
(optional)
ruler
baking sheet lined with
parchment paper
double-ended ball tool
plastic dowel pin
tissue paper
polystyrene ball about 3¼in.
in diameter or a tennis ball
icing smoother
6in. round cake board
20in. ivory ribbon, ³⁄₈in. wide
double-sided tape
pastry bag with a
no. 2 plain tip attached
paintbrushes

1 Using a long serrated knife, level the flat side of the ball cake halves to ensure they will create a neat ball shape when the flat sides are held together. Take one of the ball cake halves and cut off the domed top (a), then turn the cake cut-side down—this will form a flat, stable base for the bottom of the teapot. Place the domed ball cake on top to create a ball shape. Using a small serrated knife, trim off the top of the dome to create a level surface—this will form a flat, stable foundation for the teapot lid to sit on.

2 Using a long serrated knife, slice each cake in half horizontally to form four layers. Stack the layers back together and, if necessary, carefully trim the edge of the sponge cake with the sharp knife to neaten the ball cake and create a smooth, flat surface (b). Following the instructions on page 92, fill and cover the cake with buttercream, lightly brushing the top of each layer with sugar syrup. Chill in the refrigerator 2 hours until set.

3 Meanwhile, dust the work surface with powdered sugar, then knead the ivory modeling paste until it is soft and pliable. For the base of the teapot lid, roll out 5½oz. of the ivory modeling paste until it is ¼in. thick, using marzipan spacers, if you like. Cut out one circle about 4in. in diameter and one circle about 3¼in. in diameter. To make the tip of the teapot lid, mold ⅛oz. of the ivory modeling paste into a tear-drop shape. Place the teapot lid pieces on the prepared baking sheet.

4 To make the teapot handle, roll 1oz. of the ivory modeling paste into a sausage shape about 6in. long, then flatten the handle with the rolling pin until it is about ¼in. thick. Round off the ends of the handle with your fingers for a neat finish. Place the handle on its side on the prepared baking sheet and curve it into the desired shape (see picture on page 125).

5 For the spout, roll 1¾oz. of the ivory modeling paste into a tapered sausage about 4in. long. Flatten the wider end of the sausage to form the base of the spout, then indent a hole in the other end with the large head of the ball tool for the tip of the spout. Curve the modeling paste into a

(a)

(b)

spout shape. Using the dowel pin, indent a small hole at the base of the spout—this will help you to attach the spout to the cake, see **(j)**. Remove the dowel pin and set aside until needed. Place the spout on the prepared baking sheet and use some crumpled tissue paper to maintain it in position while it dries.

6 To make the dome of the teapot lid, roll out the remaining ivory modeling paste until it is ¼in. thick, using marzipan spacers, if you like, then cut out a circle about 4¼in. in diameter. Cover the polystyrene ball with plastic wrap, then lay the modeling paste over the top, smoothing down the sides with your hands **(c)**—this forms the concave dome when dry **(d)**. Place the polystyrene ball in the top of a drinking glass to keep the modeling paste in position while it dries. Leave all of the teapot lid pieces to dry overnight, uncovered, in a cool, dry place.

7 When the buttercream has set, remove the cake from the refrigerator. Dust the work surface with a little powdered sugar, then knead 2lb. 4oz. of the ivory gum paste until it is soft and pliable. Roll out the kneaded gum paste until it is ¼in. thick, using marzipan spacers, if you like. Lift the rolled gum paste and gently drape it over the cake, taking care not to stretch or pull it, then use your hands to smooth it over the top and side of the cake. Trim off any excess gum paste at the bottom of the cake, leaving about a ¾in. border. Gently ease the border under the cake. Smooth the gum paste again using the icing smoother. Decide which section of the cake will be the front, then concentrate on making that section look as smooth and neat as possible, hiding any creases in the gum paste at the back of the cake.

8 Dust the work surface with a little more powdered sugar, then knead the remaining ivory gum paste until it is soft and pliable. Following the instructions on page 154, cover the cake board with gum paste and line the edge with ivory ribbon, trimming it as necessary and securing the join at the back with double-sided tape. Leave the covered cake and cake board overnight, uncovered, in a cool, dry place to allow the gum paste to dry.

(c)

(d)

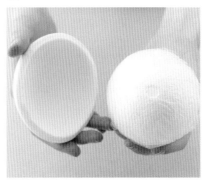

9 The next day, spoon the royal icing into the pastry bag. To assemble the lid, attach the small base circle to the center of the large base circle **(e)** with royal icing. (For hints on piping, see pages 157–9.) Turn the base upside down and attach the dome to the center of the larger circle with royal icing **(f)**. Dust the work surface with a little powdered sugar, then knead the dark blue gum paste until it is soft and pliable. Roll the gum paste into a thin sausage about 4in. long. Attach the blue trim around the base of the dome **(g)** with a little royal icing. Trim as necessary. Attach the tear-drop tip to the center of the dome at the top and secure in place with royal icing. Set the lid aside to firm up a little.

10 Put the cocoa butter beans in the center of a plate set over a bowl of just-boiled water. Put a small amount of the edible food dusts around the edge of the plate, then mix with some of the melting beans to make an edible painter's palette. Using the picture as a guide, paint a floral pattern all over the cake **(h)**. Set aside about 20 minutes, or until the pattern has dried.

11 Attach the handle to the cake with royal icing, then hold it in place a few seconds while the icing sets **(i)**. Insert the dowel into the indent in the base of the spout. Position the spout at the front of the cake, then push the dowel into the cake at a slight angle **(j)** and hold the spout in place with royal icing. Use crumpled pieces of tissue paper to support the handle and spout while they dry. Attach the lid to the top of the cake with royal icing. Allow the icing to set completely before serving.

(e)   **(f)**   **(g)**

(h)   **(i)**   **(j)**

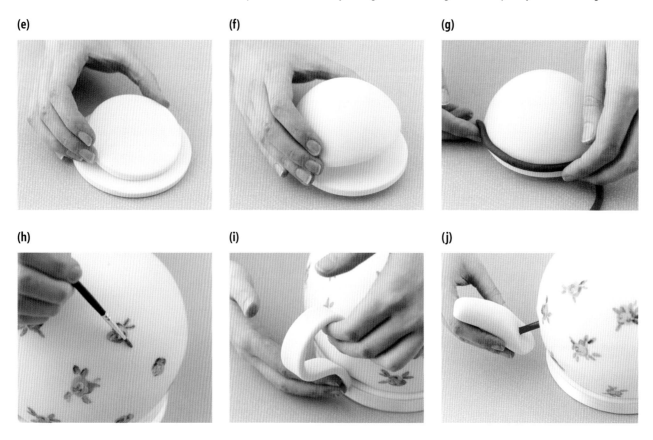

Rose Cupcakes

MAKES 6 CUPCAKES
powdered sugar, for dusting
11¼oz. white flower paste
edible glue or cooled, boiled
  water
pink edible food dust
¼ recipe quantity Vanilla
  buttercream (see page 16)
6 Vanilla or Citrus Cupcakes
  (see page 129)

YOU WILL NEED
small rolling pin
small, medium and large rose
  petal templates (see page 168)
  or 1in., 1⅓in. and 1½in. rose
  petal cutters
sharp knife
modeling pad or a clean, dry
  folded tea towel
double-ended ball tool
small paintbrush
toothpick

HINTS
You can make small or large roses
to decorate your cupcakes or a
mixture of both. Always take care
not to flatten the curved shape
of the medium and large petals
when attaching them to the roses.
If necessary, support the outer
petals of large roses while they
dry with pieces of crumpled tissue
paper or aluminum foil.

Always use dry edible dust when
coloring delicate flowers.

1 Dust the work surface with a little powdered sugar, then knead 1oz. of the flower paste until smooth and elastic. Mold ⅛oz. of the kneaded paste into a cone shape. Repeat to make six cones in total. Leave the cones to dry overnight, uncovered, in a cool, dry place.

2 When the cones have dried, dust the work surface with powdered sugar, then knead 1¾oz. of the flower paste until it is smooth and elastic. Roll out the kneaded flower paste quite thinly. Place the template for the small rose petal on the rolled flower paste and cut around it with the sharp knife to make 6 petals. Place the petals on the modeling pad, then gently roll the large head of the ball tool over each petal to soften the edges. Lightly cover the back of the first petal with edible glue, then wrap it around one of the cones to form a tight bud **(a)**. Brush the bottom half of the second petal with edible glue. Attach one side of the petal to the bud, leaving the other side unattached and slightly hanging away from the bud. Brush the bottom half of the third petal with a little edible glue. Slightly tuck one side of the third petal under the second. Gently smooth the overlap with your finger and leave the other side of the third petal unattached and slightly hanging away from the bud. Repeat with the remaining 3 petals, attaching both sides of the final petal to the bud, to form a rose bud.

3 For a small open rose, reroll the flower-paste trimmings quite thinly and cut out 9 petals with the medium rose-petal template. Place the petals on the modeling pad. Gently roll the ball tool over the center of each one to give them a curved shape, then carefully curl the top edges outward with the side of the toothpick. Following the instructions in step 2, attach the petals to the rose bud **(b)**.

4 For a large open rose, reroll the flower-paste trimmings quite thinly and cut out 6 petals using the large rose-petal template. Following the instructions in steps 2–3, attach the petals to the small rose.

5 Repeat steps 2–4 with the remaining flower paste to make six roses in total. Leave the roses to dry overnight, uncovered, at room temperature. When the roses have dried, brush the center of each one with a little pink edible food dust. Following the instructions on page 152, spread a thin layer of buttercream on top of each cupcake, then carefully place a rose on top of each one.

(a)

(b)

Mini Cakes

PREPARING ROUND MINI CAKES

MAKES 4 MINI CAKES
4in. square Rich Chocolate Cake,
    Sponge Cake or Marble Cake
    (see pages 56–7, 62–3
    or 76–7)
1 recipe quantity Sugar Syrup
    (see page 119)
½ recipe quantity Vanilla
    Buttercream or Chocolate
    Ganache (see page 16)

YOU WILL NEED
cake leveler or small serrated
    knife
2in. circle cutter
pastry brush
small angled metal spatula
4 x 2in. round cake boards

Chill the cake in the refrigerator at least 1 hour until cold and firm. Using the cake leveler, level the top of the cake, then slice it in half horizontally. From each layer, stamp out 4 circles using the 2in. circle cutter, to make 8 sponge-cake circles. Lightly brush the top of 4 of the sponge-cake circles with sugar syrup, then spread a thin layer of buttercream over the top with the angled metal spatula. Carefully place the 4 remaining plain sponge-cake circles on top of the filling to make four layered mini cakes in total. (For hints on layering and filling cakes, see page 150.) Attach the mini cakes to the cake boards with a little buttercream. Following the instructions on page 152, cover the cakes with buttercream, then chill in the refrigerator 2 hours until set. When the buttercream has set, the cakes will be ready to be covered in gum paste.

PREPARING DOME MINI CAKES

MAKES 4 MINI CAKES
4 x 3¼in. Sponge Cake or
    Marble Cake ball cake halves
    (see pages 62–3, 76–7)
1 recipe quantity Sugar Syrup
    (see page 119)
½ recipe quantity Vanilla
    Buttercream (see page 16)
4 tsp. seedless raspberry jam

YOU WILL NEED
small serrated knife
pastry brush
small angled metal spatula
4 x 3¼in. round cake boards

HINT
For hints on baking ball cake
halves, see page 92.

Level the flat side of one of the ball cake halves with the serrated knife, then slice it in half horizontally to form two layers. Lightly brush the top of the flat layer with sugar syrup, then spread a thin layer of buttercream followed by a thin layer of jam on top of each one with the angled metal spatula. Carefully place the domed layer of the cake on top of the filling to form a domed layer cake. Repeat with the remaining ball cake halves to make four layered dome cakes in total. (For hints on layering and filling cakes, see page 150.) Attach the dome cakes to the cake boards with a little buttercream. Following the instructions on page 152, cover the cakes with buttercream, then chill in the refrigerator 2 hours until set. When the buttercream has set, the cakes will be ready to be covered in gum paste.

Use this round mini cake recipe
for the following recipe:

Use this dome mini cake recipe
for the following recipe:

Magnificent Mini Cakes
page 121

Birthday Butterfly Mini Domes
page 104

Cupcakes

**MAKES 6 OR 12
CUPCAKES OR 24 MINI
CUPCAKES**
**Rich Chocolate Cake, Sponge
Cake or Marble Cake mixture
for 6 or 12 cupcakes or 24 mini
cupcakes (see pages 56–7,
62–3 or 76–7)**

YOU WILL NEED
**12-cup muffin pan or 24-cup
mini muffin pan**
**6 or 12 baking cups or
24 mini baking cups**

HINT
Remember you can make
cupcakes with a flavored
basic sponge-cake batter
too (see pages 62–3).

1 Preheat the oven to 350°F and set 6 or 12 paper baking cups in the 12-cup muffin pan or 24 mini baking cups in the 24-cup mini muffin pan. Divide your cake batter evenly between the baking cups, filling each one about two-thirds full to allow room for the cupcakes to rise.

2 Bake for the recommended time specified in the table for your chosen cake batter, or until the top of the cakes spring back slightly when gently pressed with a finger and a skewer inserted into the center comes out clean.

3 Remove the cakes from the oven and leave to cool 5 minutes, then remove from the pan, transfer to a wire rack and leave to cool completely. (For hints on covering cupcakes with buttercream, see page 152. For hints on frosting cupcakes with swirls, see page 157.)

Use this cupcake recipe for the following recipes throughout this book:

**Chocolate Swirl Mini
Cupcakes**
page 15

Rose Swirl Cupcakes
page 22

**Rose Bouquet
Cupcakes**
page 67

Mini Ghost Cakes
page 91

**Baby Shower
Cupcakes**
page 110

Rose Cupcakes
page 126

Hydrangea Cake

MAKES 1 CAKE
3 tbsp. apricot jam, warmed
8in. round Fruit Cake
    (see pages 108–9)
powdered sugar, for dusting
1lb. 14oz. marzipan
2lb. 2oz. white gum paste
    (see pages 160–1)
pale green edible food dust
green edible food dust
¼ cup white soft-peak
    Royal Icing (see page 46))

YOU WILL NEED
pastry brush
8in. round cake board
rolling pin
hydrangea cutter and veining
    mold set
indented foam pad or a piece of
    crinkled aluminum foil
small paintbrushes
pastry bag with a no. 1.5
    plain tip attached
10in. ivory ribbon, 2in. wide

HINTS
You will need to cover the cake in marzipan the day before you want to cover it with gum paste.

You will need to cover the cake in gum paste and make and mold the hydrangea flowers at least a day before they are needed.

Always use dry edible food dust when coloring delicate flowers.

1 Brush the top of the cake board with a little jam, then attach the cake upside-down to the board, to give the cake a flat top. Dust the work surface with a little powdered sugar, then knead the marzipan until it is soft, but take care not to overknead it. Fill any gaps around the base of the cake with a little of the kneaded marzipan. Following the instructions on page 153, cover the cake with the remaining kneaded marzipan. Leave to dry overnight, uncovered, in a cool, dry place. The following day, cover the cake with 1lb. 14oz. of kneaded, rolled white gum paste and leave to dry overnight.

2 Once you have covered the cake with gum paste, make the hydrangeas. Dust the work surface with a little more powdered sugar, then knead the remaining white gum paste until it is soft and pliable. Roll out the kneaded gum paste quite thinly. Stamp out a hydrangea using the hydrangea cutter, then immediately place it into the veining mold and gently bring the sides of the mold together. Place the veined hydrangea flower on the indented foam pad—this will help the flower to keep its curved shape as it dries. Stamping and molding one hydrangea at a time, repeat with the remaining gum paste to make 50 flowers in total, rerolling the gum paste as necessary. Leave the flowers to dry overnight, uncovered, in a cool, dry place.

3 When the gum paste has set and the flowers have dried, brush the center of each flower with pale green edible food dust, then brush a tiny amount of green edible food dust on top in the very center of the flower. Spoon the royal icing into the pastry bag and pipe a small dot of icing in the center of each flower. Leave the flowers at least 2 hours, uncovered, in a cool, dry place to allow the icing to set.

4 Meanwhile, wrap the ribbon around the bottom of the cake, securing the join at the back with a little royal icing and trimming as necessary. Leave to dry completely. Roll up the pastry bag and store in an airtight container until needed.

5 When the flowers have dried, attach them in a random fashion over the top and side of the cake, securing each one with a dot of royal icing.

Flower Cake Pops

MAKES 12 CAKE POPS
powdered sugar, for dusting
1oz. yellow-colored gum paste
  (see pages 160–1)
2¼oz. white gum paste
  (see pages 160–1)
2 tbsp. white soft-peak Royal
  Icing (see page 46)
2 tbsp. pale green-colored soft-
  peak Royal Icing (see page 46)
2 tbsp. yellow-colored soft-peak
  royal icing (see page 46)
6in. Basic Sponge Cake
  (see pages 62–3)
½ recipe quantity Vanilla
  Frosting (see page 118)
9oz. yellow confectionery
  coating

YOU WILL NEED
small rolling pin
½in. blossom plunger cutter
¾in. daisy plunger cutter
modeling pad or a clean,
  dry folded tea towel
3 pastry bags
baking sheet lined with
  parchment paper
12 paper lollipop sticks
11ft. multicolored ribbon,
  1¼in. wide, cut into 12 equal
  pieces (optional)

HINT
You will need to make the gum-
paste flowers and the sponge cake
for the moist cake mix at least a
day before they are needed.

1 To make the small blossom flowers, dust the work surface with a little powdered sugar, then knead the yellow gum paste until it is soft and pliable. Roll out the kneaded gum paste quite thinly and stamp out 36 small blossoms using the ½in. blossom plunger cutter. Repeat with 1oz. of the white gum paste to make 72 blossoms in total. To make the daisies, dust the work surface with a little more powdered sugar, then knead the remaining white gum paste until it is soft and pliable. Roll out the kneaded gum paste quite thinly and stamp out 36 daisies using the ¾in. daisy plunger cutter. Carefully transfer the blossoms and the daisies to the modeling pad and leave to dry overnight, uncovered, in a cool, dry place.

2 When the flowers have dried, spoon the white soft-peak royal icing into one of the pastry bags, then snip off the pointed end if necessary. Pipe a dot of icing in the center of the small yellow blossoms. Repeat with the remaining soft peak royal icings and pipings bags, piping a dot of pale green icing into the center of the small white blossoms and a dot of yellow icing into the center of the daisies. Leave the flowers at least 2 hours, uncovered, in a cool, dry place to set.

3 When the icing has set, follow the instructions in step 1 on page 68 and make a moist cake mixture using the sponge cake and frosting. Divide the mixture into 12 equally sized balls, smoothing the surface of each one with your fingers, then transfer them to the prepared tray. Chill the cake pops in the refrigerator about 1 hour until firm. Alternatively, freeze the cake pops about 15 minutes until hard.

4 Put the confectionery coating in a heatproof bowl and rest it over a saucepan of gently simmering water, making sure the bottom of the bowl does not touch the water. Heat, stirring occasionally, until melted. Alternatively, put the confectionery coating in a bowl and microwave, uncovered, on medium 2 minutes until melted, stirring every 30 seconds to ensure the coating does not overheat. The confectionery coating should have a smooth pouring consistency similar to heavy cream.

5 Dip the tip of one of the lollipop sticks about ½in. into the melted confectionery coating and gently push it into the base of one of the cake pops until the coated tip is hidden from view. Holding the end of the lollipop stick, gently twist the cake pop through the confectionery coating until it is completely coated, using a teaspoon to help if necessary. Lift the cake pop out of the confectionery coating, allowing any excess coating to fall back in to the bowl. Transfer the coated cake pop to a drinking glass to hold it upright. Working quickly before the coating hardens, attach a few daisies and a few blossoms to the coated cake pop and leave to set at least 10 to 15 minutes. Repeat with the remaining lollipop sticks, cake pops, confectionery coating and gum-paste flowers until all the cake pops are coated and decorated, reheating the confectionery coating if necessary. When the confectionery coating has completely set, tie a ribbon around each lollipop stick and finish with a bow, if you like.

Gift-Wrapped Cake

MAKES 1 CAKE
2 x 6in. square Marble Cakes (see pages 76–7)
1¼ cups Basic Buttercream (see page 16)
powdered sugar, for dusting
1lb. 5oz. white gum paste (see pages 160–1)
2½oz. white modeling paste (see pages 160–1)
edible glue or cooled, boiled water
2 tbsp. orange-colored soft-peak Royal Icing (see page 46)
8 x 11in. gum paste transfer sheet
¼ cup white soft-peak Royal Icing (see page 46)

YOU WILL NEED
6in. square cake board
small rolling pin
bow templates (see page 165)
sharp knife
design wheeler tool
baking sheet lined with parchment paper
small paintbrush
tissue paper
⅝in. and 1in. primrose flower plunger cutters
indented foam pad or a piece of crinkled aluminum foil
2 pastry bags, each with a no. 2 plain tip attached
ruler

HINT
Gum paste sheets are widely available online in a variety of designs and colors. You can even draw your own design and send it to a company that can transfer it onto a sheet of gum paste.

1 Following the instructions on page 150 and using the cake board as a firm base, layer the cakes, then fill with buttercream to make one tall 6in. cake. Following the instructions on page 152, cover the cake with the remaining buttercream. Chill in the refrigerator 2 hours. When the buttercream has set, dust the work surface with a little powdered sugar and knead the white gum paste until it is soft and pliable. Following the instructions on page 153, cover the cake with the kneaded gum paste.

2 Dust the work surface with a little more powdered sugar, then knead 1¾oz. of the white modeling paste until it is soft and pliable. Then roll it out quite thinly. Place the templates for the bow on top of the rolled modeling paste and cut around them with the sharp knife then use the design wheeler tool to indent a "stitched" line along the edges of each strip. Transfer the pieces to the prepared baking sheet. Pinch together the plain end of each tail piece, then mold the modeling paste to give the tail pieces a slight curve (see picture). Take one of the loop pieces and brush one of the short ends with a little edible glue, then fold it in half to form a loop, pinching it in slightly at the join. Repeat with the remaining loop piece to make 2 loops. Stuff the hollow of each loop with a small piece of crumpled tissue paper—this will keep the modeling paste in position while it dries. To assemble the bow, arrange the loops and tail pieces in position on the prepared baking sheet, then mold the bow join over the top to hide the point where the pieces meet, securing the pieces in place with a little edible glue.

3 Dust the work surface with a little more powdered sugar and knead the remaining white modeling paste until it is soft and pliable. Roll out the kneaded modeling paste quite thinly, then stamp out 12 primrose flowers using the ⅝in. primrose plunger cutter. Roll the trimmings into a ball and repeat with the 1in. primrose plunger cutter to make 6 larger primrose flowers. Place all of the flowers on the indented foam pad—this will help the flowers to keep their curved shape as they dry. Leave the cake, bow and flowers overnight, uncovered, in a cool, dry place to allow the gum and modeling pastes to dry.

4 The next day, spoon the orange soft-peak royal icing into one of the pastry bags and pipe a dot of icing into the center of each flower. Leave to one side to allow the icing to set. Meanwhile, cut the gum paste transfer sheet into 4 strips, each one about 7 x 2½in. Peel off the plastic backing from one of the strips, carefully sliding the sharp knife between the sheet and the backing. Brush the back of the strip with edible glue and position it in the center of one side of the cake. Lining it up squarely at the base, gently smooth it over the side and top of the cake—you'll need to work quickly or the strip will dry out and become brittle. Working with one strip at a time, repeat with the remaining strips and edible glue until all the strips meet in the middle to create a "ribbon-wrapped" effect. Spoon the white royal icing into the remaining pastry bag, then pipe small dots of icing along the edges of each strip. Attach the bow to the top of the cake, then attach the primrose flowers randomly over the "ribbon," securing the elements in place with a little royal icing.

Daisy Chain Mouse Cake

MAKES 1 CAKE
2 x 4in. round Marble Cakes
  (see pages 76–7)
½ recipe quantity Vanilla
  Buttercream (see page 16)
powdered sugar, for dusting
14oz. pale green-colored gum
  paste (see pages 160–1)
2½oz. white modeling paste
  (see pages 160–1)
¾oz. pale pink-colored modeling
  paste (see pages 160–1)
¾oz. purple-colored modeling
  paste (see pages 160–1)
¼oz. dark green-colored
  modeling or gum paste
  (see pages 160–1)
¼oz. pale yellow-colored
  modeling or gum paste
  (see pages 160–1)
edible glue or cooled, boiled
  water
piece of dry spaghetti (optional)
black food paste coloring

YOU WILL NEED
4in. round cake board
sharp knife
small rolling pin
2½in. 6-petal flower cutter
small paintbrush
ruler
double-ended ball tool
  (optional)
¾in. daisy plunger cutter
indented foam pad or a piece of
  crinkled aluminum foil
15in. lilac ribbon, ⅜in. wide

HINT
You will need to make the cake,
the mouse and the daisies at least
a day before they are needed.

1 Following the instructions on page 150 and using the cake board as a firm base, layer the cakes, then fill with buttercream to make one tall 4in. cake. Following the instructions on page 152, cover the cake with the remaining buttercream. Chill in the refrigerator 2 hours.

2 When the buttercream has set, remove the cake from the refrigerator. Dust the work surface with a little powdered sugar, then knead the pale green gum paste until it is soft and pliable. Following the instructions on page 153, cover the cake with the kneaded gum paste.

3 Knead all of the modeling pastes until they are soft and pliable. To make the mouse's head, mold ¼oz. of the white modeling paste into a tear-drop shape and leave to firm up a little. To make the feet, mold 2 pea-sized tear-drop shapes of white modeling paste. Indent the toes with the sharp knife, then slightly flatten the back of the feet to make a flat base for the body to rest on. Leave the feet to dry overnight, uncovered, in a cool, dry place. To make the lower body, mold 1oz. of the white modeling paste into a tear-drop shape, then flatten it slightly at the top and bottom.

4 For the skirt of the dress, roll out ½oz. of the pale pink modeling paste quite thinly and cut out a flower using the 6-petal flower cutter. Repeat using the same amount of purple modeling paste to make a purple flower. Using a small amount of edible glue to secure each layer, lay the pale pink flower over the top of the lower body **(a)**, followed by the purple flower.

5 For the upper body, roll ⅛oz. of the white modeling paste into an oval, then gently press the top to flatten slightly. Push a small piece of dry spaghetti through the centre of the upper body. Brush the base of the upper body with a little edible glue, then attach it to the skirt, pushing the dry spaghetti

through the center of the skirt as you do so **(b)**—this will support the upper body and head. Trim the dry spaghetti, if necessary.

6 For the arms, roll 2 pea-sized balls of white modeling paste into thin sausages and lightly pinch them in at the wrists. Flatten the hands slightly and indent a couple of lines with the sharp knife for fingers. Attach the arms to the top of the body with edible glue **(c)**.

7 For the dress straps, roll a pea-sized ball of purple modeling paste into a very thin sausage and cut it into 2 pieces, each about 1¼in. long. For the front of the dress, roll out the remaining purple modeling paste quite thinly and cut a rectangle about 1 x ½in. Using edible glue, attach the straps to the upper body, followed by the front of the dress.

8 Brush the base of the head with edible glue and attach to the upper body, inserting the center of the head onto the dry spaghetti **(d)**.

9 To make the ears, roll a little white modeling paste into 2 pea-sized balls and indent the center of each one with the small head of the ball tool or with the tip of your little finger. For the pink centers, roll 2 tiny balls of pale pink modeling paste and flatten them slightly. Attach the pink centers

(a)   **(b)**

(c)   **(d)**

to the ears, then attach the ears to the head, securing both with edible glue. For the nose, roll a tiny ball of pale pink modeling paste and attach it to the head with edible glue. For the eyes, put a little black food paste coloring in a small bowl. Dilute with 1–2 drops of water, then carefully paint the eyes onto the mouse's face **(e)**.

10 For the tail, roll a large pea-sized ball of white modeling paste into a thin, tapering sausage. Mold the tail into the shape you would like it to have on the finished cake but do not attach it to the mouse yet. Place it on a flat surface and leave it to dry overnight, uncovered, in a cool, dry place.

11 To make the daisy stalks, roll out the dark green modeling paste into a long, very thin sausage and cut it into 8 pieces, each about 1in. long. Attach 1 stalk to one of the mouse's hands with a little edible glue. Place the remaining daisy stalks on a flat surface, curving each one slightly as you do so. Leave the daisy stalks to dry overnight, uncovered, in a cool, dry place.

12 Roll out the remaining white modeling paste quite thinly and stamp out at least 8 daisies using the daisy plunger cutter. Roll out at least 8 tiny balls of the pale yellow modeling paste and attach each one to the center of a daisy with a little edible glue. Place the daisies on the indented foam pad—this will help them take on a slightly curved shape when they dry. Leave the daisies, mouse and gum-paste covered cake to dry overnight, uncovered, in a cool, dry place.

13 When all the elements have dried, assemble the cake. Place the mouse's feet onto the cake. Hold them in place with a little edible glue. Brush the flattened sides of the feet and the bottom of the mouse's body with edible glue and carefully rest the body on top of the feet. Position the tail and attach it with a little edible glue **(f)**. Attach one of the daisies to the end of the stalk in the mouse's hand **(g)**. Set the rest of the stalks and daisies on top of the cake and trailing down the side to create a daisy chain, securing with edible glue. Wrap the ribbon around the bottom of the cake, securing the join at the back with a little edible glue and trimming as necessary. Leave to dry completely.

(e)

(f)

(g)

CHAPTER FIVE

It's time to reveal my best-kept secrets! Baking and decorating can take a lot of preparation, but with a little know-how you'll be able to make delicious decorated treats with ease. From tools and equipment to techniques and templates, you'll find everything you need and more in this chapter to create beautiful baked goodies time and time again.

BEST-KEPT
SECRETS

Basic Equipment

The following basic items will all be very useful when you are making, baking and frosting the cakes and icing the cookies in this book. Items needed for specific projects are listed on the recipe pages. You'll probably find that you already own a lot of the equipment listed in the baking section. Cookie cutters used in specific recipes can be replaced by templates, especially if you only have to cut out a small number of shapes (see pages 162–171). For larger quantities, however, I do recommend purchasing cookie cutters. They are inexpensive and widely available.

The equipment listed in the icing and decorating sections is extremely useful, especially if you intend to make lots of cakes and cookies. The cake leveler, for instance, is a particularly handy tool that will allow you to level and split your sponge cakes quickly and easily, but a long serrated knife can always be used instead. Other items like plunger cutters will make your life much easier when trying to create large quantities of small gum-paste decorations—a task that could feel insurmountable if attempted by hand.

Now that so many of us are starting to be more creative with our cake making, you'll find that all of the equipment listed is readily available. I have listed a few well-known online suppliers on page 172.

BAKING EQUIPMENT

Baking pans

(1) Baking sheets

(2) Ball pans

(3) Cake pans (in a range of different shapes and sizes)

(4) Ceramic baking beans

(5) Circle cutters (½–3¼in. in diameter)

(6) Cookie cutters

(7) Cooling racks

Electric mixers—a stand mixer or hand-held electric mixer with beater and whisk attachments will make preparing your cake batter and cookie dough much easier.

(8) Foil or paper baking cups

Kitchen scales—ideally digital for accuracy.

(9) Metal spatula (large)—used to transfer hot, freshly baked cookies from the oven onto cooling racks.

(10) Mixing bowls/Heatproof bowls

(11) Muffin pans (12-cup and 24-cup)

Parchment paper

(12) Rolling pin (large)

(13) Sieve

(14) Spatula—used for mixing and spreading. Spatulas with a broad, flexible plastic or silicone blade are ideal for these jobs.

Spring-action release ice-cream scoop—used to measure out whoopie pie mixture before baking. Scoops are a foolproof way to ensure you end up with an even batch.

(15) Wooden spoon

ICING EQUIPMENT

(1) Angled metal spatulas—a large angled metal spatula is used to add fillings to cakes and to assist you when stacking cake tiers. A small angled metal spatula is used to lift small amounts of gum paste onto cookies to prevent the gum paste from stretching.

(2) Cake boards—used to stabilize tiered cakes and ensure that the plastic dowel rods do not penetrate the layer above. They make any cake easy to transport. Normally silver in color, they can also be covered in gum paste and used as a decorative base to complement your finished cake. For an elegant finish, use the same color of gum paste to cover the board that you used to cover the cake. For a dramatic finish, use a contrasting color.

(3) Cake cards (also referred to as boards)—make it easier to move cakes into position onto plates or cake stands and are particularly handy for mini cakes. They are slightly thinner than cake boards but can also be used to stabilize tiered cakes.

(4) Cake leveler (also called a cake slicer)—used to level and split sponge cakes (not suitable for use on fruit cakes). It has a variable height adjustment for cutting layers to the desired depth.

Cake turntable—used when decorating the sides of a cake. Tiltable turntables are ideal for this job.

Carpenter's level (small)—used when leveling and layering cakes. Ensuring your cake has a level top early on in the process means that it is less likely to tilt during the stacking process. Not to be stored in the toolbox!

(5) Dipping forks—used for dipping chocolates and truffles in melted coatings; 2- or 3-pronged dipping forks are also extremely helpful when dipping fancies in fondant icing.

Doweling guide—used to mark the position of the dowel rods to be inserted into the tiers of a stacked cake (see page 171).

(6) Dowel rods—used to support cake tiers from collapsing into the tier below and should be used in conjunction with a cake board. Dowel rods are usually made of plastic and should be cut to the correct length with a strong pair of scissors or clippers.

(7) Icing smoothers—used to achieve a smooth, flat surface after covering cakes with gum paste or marzipan. They will help you to achieve a perfect, professional finish.

(8) Icing tips—used for piping frosting onto cupcakes and to pipe fillings onto macarons and whoopie pies. I usually use $5/8$in. closed-star, open-star and plain tips.

(9) Marzipan spacers—are used when rolling out gum paste, fondant, marzipan or cookie dough to give you an even thickness. I usually use ¼in. spacers.

(10) Metal side scraper—used to achieve a smooth, even finish after covering the sides of a cake in buttercream or chocolate ganache.

(11) Paper lollipop sticks—inserted into cake pops or the base of cupcakes. They can also be pushed into raw cookie dough prior to baking, to create cookies on sticks.

(12) Pastry bags—used for piping large amounts of buttercream, frosting or meringue. Large, disposable or heavy-duty synthetic pastry bags are ideal for this job.

(13) Pastry brush—used to brush sugar syrup on sponge cakes.

(14) Plastic squeeze bottles—used for squeezing flood-consistency royal icing onto the surface of cookies. Using a squeeze bottle enables you to control exactly where you want the icing to go in the correct quantity. This is a handy piece of equipment for the cookie projects in this book.

(15) Rolling pin (small)—used for rolling out gum paste, flower paste and modeling paste.

(16) Ruler—used for measuring rolled-out gum paste when specific sizes need to be cut. Metal rulers are ideal for this job.

(17) Sharp knife—used to achieve a clean finish when cutting out marzipan, cookie dough and gum paste, flower paste and modeling paste.

(18) Spring-action-release ice-cream scoop—used to measure out truffle mixture to ensure you end up with an even batch.

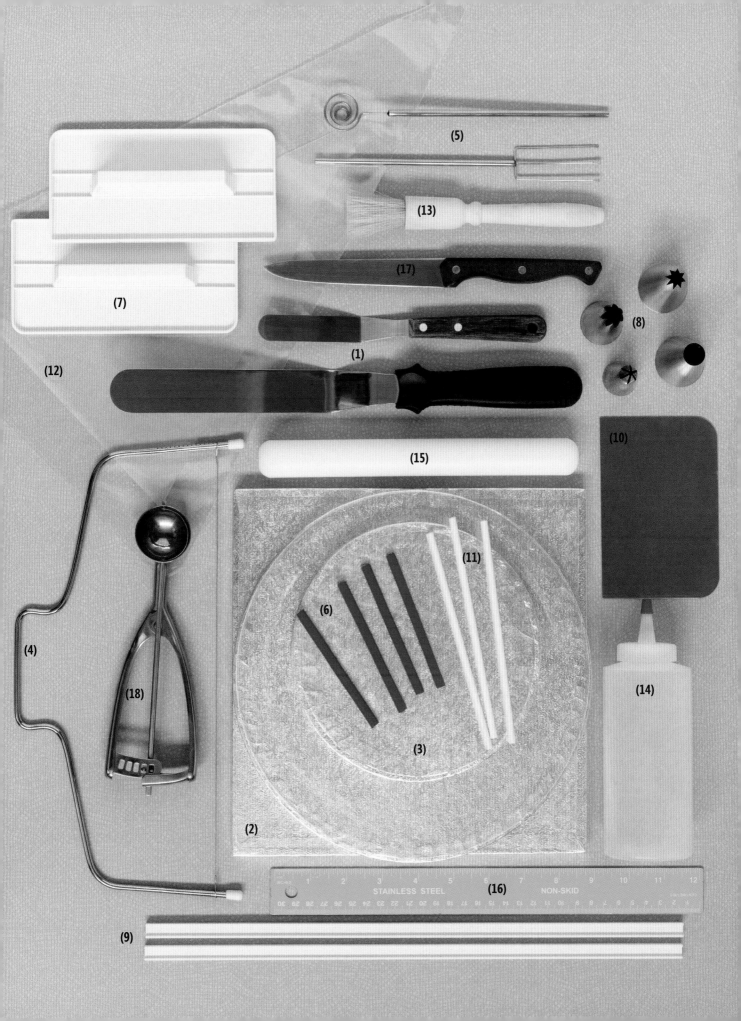

DECORATING EQUIPMENT

Tools

(1) Ball tool (double-headed)—an essential tool, used to shape the petals of sugar flowers, for round indentations and for adding detail to gum-paste decorations.

(2) Craft knife—a small, sharp-bladed knife used when working with gum-paste sheets or chocolate transfers, or for intricate sugarcraft work.

(3) Decorating tips—the no. 2 and the no. 1.5 plain tips are used for piping royal icing onto cookies or to add intricate details onto cakes and cookies.

(4) Design wheeler tool—a detailing tool used to create pattern designs on gum paste, flower paste or modeling paste. It has three interchangeable heads: fluted, stitch and rounded wheel. The stitch head is used in several of the projects in this book.

(5) Gum-paste cutters—made of either steel or plastic and available in a huge range of flower and leaf shapes. For use with rolled-out gum paste, modeling paste or flower paste.

(6) Hydrangea cutter and veining mold set—consisting of a steel flower cutter and a veining mold, this invaluable set will help you create realistic hydrangea flowers with ease.

(7) Indented foam pad—a curvy, sponge pad on which to leave gum-paste flowers or leaves to dry overnight. It allows the edges of your leaves and flowers to dry with a slight curved shape to give sugarcraft creations a more natural appearance.

(8) Leaf veiner or veining mold—lightly rolling the mold over the top of the leaf gives gum-paste leaves a more natural look.

(9) Modeling pad—a flat, foam pad used in conjunction with a ball tool (see above) to give gum-paste flowers a more natural look.

(10) Molds—a selection of delicate silicone molds used to create detailed gum- and modeling-paste decorations for cakes, cupcakes or cookies. Sugarcraft molds come in a vast array of shapes and designs. Gum paste or modeling paste is pushed into the mold, then turned out and left to dry.

(11) Paintbrushes—used when handpainting intricate details onto cakes and gum- or modeling-paste models, and for brushing edible glue onto cakes and cookies and sugarcraft decorations.

Pastry bags—used to pipe royal icing details onto cakes and cookies. Small disposable or homemade pastry bags are ideal.

(12) Plunger cutters—either plain or embossed, these tools create quick and easy shapes from rolled-out gum paste or flower paste.

(13) Scriber—used to indent patterns or dots or to transfer a design onto gum paste. It is also useful for popping any air bubbles that may appear in the gum paste when covering cakes.

(14) Stencils—culinary stencils made from food-grade plastic. Used with royal icing or edible dusts or powders, they are an extremely effective way to add patterns to cakes and cookies.

(15) Straight frill cutters—used to stamp out a range of basic border designs from rolled-out gum or modeling paste.

(16) Veiner tool—used to create a vein pattern on sugarcraft flowers or leaves.

Edible Decorations

(17) Candy pearls—edible pearl beads used to add a decorative, edible element to your cake or cookies. Available in various colors.

Edible colors—edible pastes and dusts come in a huge range of colors. Pastes can be used to color fondant, gum paste, flower paste and modeling paste, buttercream, royal icing and marzipan. Dusts are used to add color accents to dried sugarcraft decorations.

(18) Edible glitter/lustre dusts—nontoxic glitters can be used to add sparkle to your creations. Dry lustre dusts can be brushed onto gum-paste decorations to create a shimmering glow, or they can be mixed with water to make an edible paint.

(19) Pen with edible ink—useful for adding small details to gum-paste models if you don't have any edible paint. They are also ideal for marking the position of dowel rods when stacking cakes.

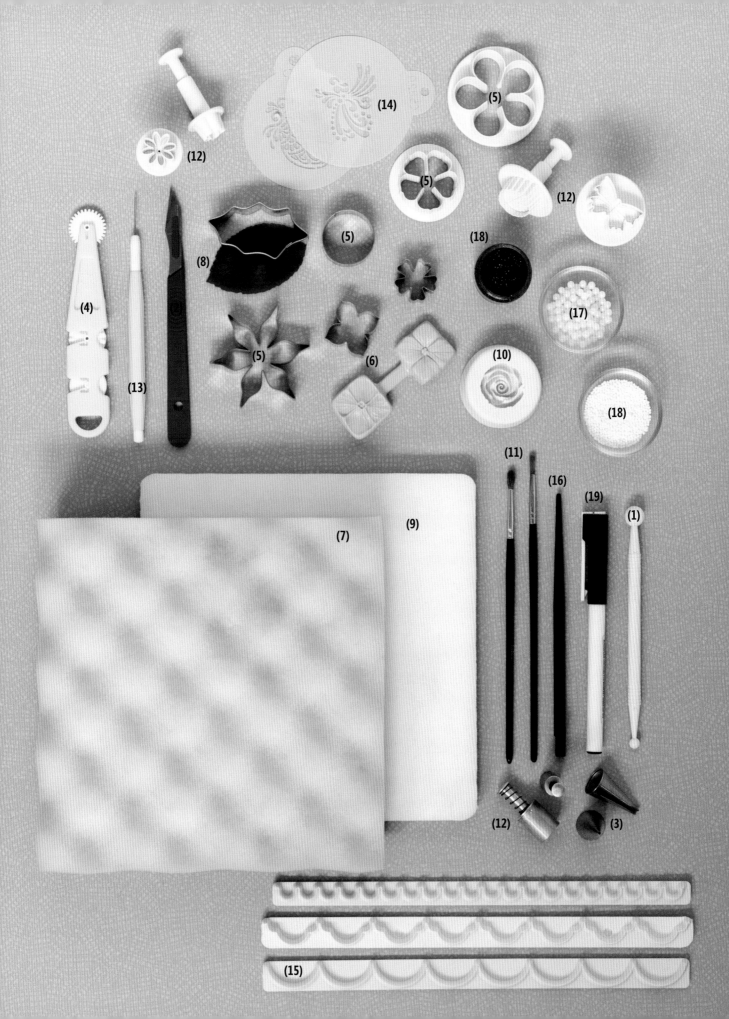

Preparing Cookies for Baking

1 recipe quantity Cookie Dough of your choice (see pages 26–7)

YOU WILL NEED
parchment paper
2 baking sheets
rolling pin
¼in. marzipan spacers (optional)
cookie template or cookie cutter
sharp knife
large metal spatula

HINTS
If you want to make your own template, draw your design onto a piece of thin cardboard and cut out the template. Place this on the rolled-out dough then cut around it using a knife. Alternatively, use a cookie cutter.

If the dough has been out of the refrigerator a long time during the cutting-out process, put it back in the refrigerator and leave it to firm up a while before baking.

1 Roll the dough into a ball, then divide it in half. Tightly seal half of the dough in plastic wrap and chill in the refrigerator until needed. Cut 4 sheets of parchment paper slightly larger than a baking sheet. Place one of the sheets of parchment paper on the work surface, then set the remaining dough in the center of the sheet **(a)**.

2 Place another sheet of parchment paper on the top of the dough, then, using the rolling pin, roll out the dough until it is about ¼in. thick, using marzipan spacers if you like **(b)**. Slide the dough, still within the sheets of parchment paper, onto one of the baking sheets. Remove the chilled ball of dough from the refrigerator and repeat as above, then stack the baking sheets on top of each other and chill in the refrigerator at least 2 hours or overnight to allow the dough to firm up before cutting. If the dough is soft during the cutting-out process, the cookies will not hold their shape well.

3 When the dough is firm, remove one of the baking sheets from the refrigerator and slide the dough, still within the sheets of parchment paper, onto the work surface. Reline the baking sheet with a fresh piece of parchment paper and set aside. Gently remove the top sheet of parchment paper from the dough and reserve until needed.

4 Place a cookie template on top of the rolled dough and cut around it as often as required **(c)**, leaving as little space as possible between the shapes. Roll the trimmings into a ball, then set the reserved sheet of parchment paper on top. Reroll the dough and cut out more cookies as above until all the dough has been used up.

5 Using the metal spatula, transfer the cookies to the lined baking sheet, spacing them 1¼in apart to allow each one to spread slightly during baking. Chill the cut-out cookies in the refrigerator while you repeat steps 3 and 4 with the remaining rolled dough.

(a)

(b)

(c)

Lining Cake Pans

butter, softened, for greasing

YOU WILL NEED
cake pan
parchment paper
pencil
scissors
ruler

LINING ROUND AND HEART-SHAPED PANS

1 First line the bottom of the pan. Set the cake pan on a sheet of parchment paper and draw around it with the pencil. Cut out the shape along the inside of the line so that the circle or heart shape fits neatly into the bottom of the pan, then set the cut-out parchment aside until needed.

2 To line the inside wall of the pan, cut out a strip of parchment paper that is long enough to cover the outside wall of the pan with a small overlap, and at least 2in. higher than the side of the pan. Fold one of the long edges of the strip up by 1in. and make a firm crease. Open out the fold, then cut little vertical slits all the way along the folded edge up to the crease, creating a frilled strip.

3 Grease the inside of the cake pan with butter, then gently press the frilled strip of parchment paper into the pan, allowing the frilled edge to sit on the bottom of the pan. Set the circle or heart piece of parchment paper into the bottom of the pan, covering the frilled strip.

LINING SQUARE PANS

Follow steps 1 and 2 as above. Grease the inside of the cake pan with butter, then gently press the frilled strip of parchment paper into the pan, allowing the frilled edge to sit on the bottom of the pan. Overlap the frills in each corner to allow the parchment paper to fit neatly into the corners of the pan, then run your finger up and down the corner edges to create 4 sharp creases—this will ensure the cake will have sharp, precise corners when you remove it from the pan. Set the square piece of parchment paper in the bottom of the pan, covering the frilled strip.

LINING BALL CAKE PANS

1 Cut out a circle of parchment paper with a diameter about 2in. wider than the diameter of the cups that form the ball pan. Cut 3 slits halfway toward the center of the circle, evenly spacing them around the side.

2 Grease one of the cups in the ball pan with butter, then place the parchment paper circle into the cup. Repeat as necessary.

Layering & Filling Cakes

FOR SPONGE CAKE, RICH CHOCOLATE CAKE OR MARBLE CAKE
1 or 2 Rich Chocolate Cakes, Sponge Cakes or Marble Cakes (see pages 56–7, 62–3 or 76–7)
Buttercream and/or seedless raspberry jam or Chocolate Ganache (see page 16)
Sugar Syrup (see page 119)

YOU WILL NEED
cake leveler or long serrated knife and a ruler
parchment paper
cake card or cake board
angled metal spatula
pastry brush

HINTS
For a tall layered sponge cake, bake two cakes and layer all four cakes together.

Ideally, make the cake(s) the day before you need to layer and fill them to prevent them from crumbling when cut. If time is short, chill the cake(s) in the refrigerator at least 2 hours before leveling and layering them.

Whenever you need to layer and fill a sponge cake, rich chocolate cake or marble cake, follow the method below using the quantity of sugar syrup and fillings specified by a particular recipe or by the charts on page 155 to achieve perfect results.

1 Using the cake leveler, level the top of the cake(s) **(a)**, then cut the cake(s) in half horizontally **(b)**. Alternatively, use a serrated knife and a ruler to level and cut the cake(s) in half.

2 Cut a piece of parchment paper slightly larger than the cake board. Set the piece of parchment paper on the work surface and place the cake board on top—this will make it easier to turn the cake when filling. Spread a very thin layer of buttercream all over the cake board, then carefully place the first layer of cake over the top—the buttercream will anchor the cake to the board.

3 If layering and filling one cake, lightly brush the top of the first layer with sugar syrup, then spread a thin layer of buttercream on top with the angled metal spatula, followed by a thin layer of jam on top of that, if using. Carefully place the second layer of the cake on top of the first, then gently press the layers together with your hands to secure them.

If layering and filling two cakes, lightly brush the top of the first layer with sugar syrup, then spread a thin layer of buttercream over the top with the angled metal spatula. Carefully place the second layer of cake on top of the first. Lightly brush the top of the second layer with sugar syrup and spread a thin layer of buttercream, or jam if preferred, on top of that **(c)**. Carefully place the third layer of the cake on top of the second, then lightly brush with sugar syrup and spread a thin layer of buttercream on top of that. Carefully place the fourth layer on top, then gently press the layers together with your hands to secure them.

(a)

(b)

(c)

Covering Fancies in Fondant Icing

FOR FONDANT FANCIES
marizpan-topped fancies
(see page 18)
freshly made fondant icing
(see page 18)

YOU WILL NEED
wire rack
parchment paper
dipping fork or table fork
foil or paper baking cups

HINT
When arranging the fancies in a tight square, ensure the sides of the cakes are touching—this will help the baking cups hold their square shape while the icing dries.

Whenever you need to cover fancies in fondant icing, simply follow the method below using the quantity of prepared fancies and fondant icing specified by the recipe.

1 Place a wire rack over a sheet of parchment paper and remove the marzipan-topped fancies from the refrigerator. Cover one cake at a time. Carefully dip one of the fancies marzipan-side down into the fondant icing until the fondant covers about three-quarters of each side **(a)**. Using a dipping fork, carefully lift the fancy out of the fondant, allowing any excess icing to drip back into the bowl **(b)**, then immediately transfer the dipped fancy to the prepared rack. Repeat with the remaining fancies then leave them all to dry 10 minutes. Store any unused fondant icing in an airtight container until needed.

2 After 10 minutes, carefully place each fancy into a baking cup **(c)**, then mold the round baking cup around the square cake, pinching the baking cup into 4 corners as you do so **(d)**. Arrange the fancies in a tight square and leave to dry until the fondant icing has completely set.

(a)   **(b)**

(c)   **(d)**

Covering Cakes with Buttercream or Chocolate Ganache

Whenever you need to cover a cake or cupcake in buttercream or chocolate ganache, simply follow the method below using the quantity of buttercream or ganache specified by a particular recipe or by the chart on page 155 to achieve perfect results.

FOR CAKES

FOR 1 CAKE
1 or 2 layered and filled cake(s) (see page 150)
Buttercream or Chocolate Ganache (see page 16)

YOU WILL NEED
parchment paper
large angled metal spatula
metal side scraper

1 Cut a piece of parchment paper slightly larger than the cake board or base of the cake. Set the piece of parchment paper on the work surface then place the cake on top—this will make it easier to turn the cake when covering. Using the angled metal spatula, cover the side of the cake with buttercream or ganache **(a)**, working smoothly and neatly until the side is completely covered in a thin, even layer. Make sure the covering on the side of the cake is smooth and even by gently running the side scraper along the side of the cake **(b)**, slowly turning the cake as you do so.

2 Holding the angled metal spatula at a slight angle, spread a thin, even layer of buttercream or ganache over the top of the cake, taking care to keep the top edge neat. Make sure the covering on top of the cake is smooth and even by gently running the side scraper over the top.

FOR CUPCAKES

FOR 1 CUPCAKE
Buttercream or Chocolate Ganache (see page 16)
cupcake (see page 129), baked in a paper or foil baking cup

YOU WILL NEED
small angled metal spatula

Put a little buttercream or ganache on the tip of the angled metal spatula and spread it onto the center of a cupcake. Spread the topping over the top of the cupcake, pushing it toward the edges of the baking cup and adding more buttercream or ganache as necessary. For a textured finish, spread the topping over the cake in circular motions with the flat tip of the angled metal spatula, indenting the topping slightly as you do so to create subtle peaks **(c)**. For a smooth finish, spread the topping over the cake in circular motions with the flat tip of the angled metal spatula, taking care not to indent the topping.

(a)

(b)

(c)

Covering Cakes with Gum Paste and Marzipan

Whenever you need to cover a cake with gum paste (or with marzipan and gum paste), simply follow the method below using the quantities specified by a particular recipe or by the chart on page 155. If you are new to covering cakes, start with slightly more gum paste or marzipan than specified so you have plenty to work with.

FOR 1 CAKE
powdered sugar, for dusting
gum paste
1 covered Rich Chocolate Cake, Sponge Cake, Marble Cake or Fruit Cake (see pages 56–7, 62–3, 76–7)

YOU WILL NEED
rolling pin
¼in. marzipan spacers (optional)
2 icing smoothers
sharp knife
scriber or sharp needle

IN ADDITION TO THE ABOVE
apricot jam, warmed, or buttercream
marzipan

YOU WILL NEED
pastry brush or angled metal spatula

COVERING CAKES WITH GUM PASTE

Dust the work surface with a little powdered sugar, then knead the gum paste until it is soft and pliable. Roll out the kneaded gum paste until it is ¼in. thick, using marzipan spacers if you like. Carefully lift the rolled gum paste and gently drape it over the top and side(s) of the cake, taking care not to stretch or pull it. Use your hands to smooth it over the top and side(s) of the cake, making sure to smooth out any air bubbles **(a)**. For a flat, smooth finish, smooth the top and side(s) of the cake again with icing smoothers **(b)**. Trim off any excess gum paste at the base of the cake with the sharp knife **(c).** Use the scriber to prick out any remaining air bubbles in the gum paste.

COVERING CAKES WITH MARZIPAN AND GUM PASTE

If covering a fruit cake, lightly brush the top and side(s) of the cake with a thin layer of apricot jam using a pastry brush. If using a sponge cake, lightly cover the top and side(s) of the cake with a thick layer of buttercream using the angled metal spatula. Dust the work surface with a little powdered sugar, then knead the marzipan until it has just softened—take care not to overknead the marzipan because this will make it oily. Roll out the kneaded marzipan until it is ¼in. thick, using marzipan spacers if you like, and cover the cake as above. Leave the cake overnight, uncovered, in a cool, dry place to allow the marzipan to set. When the marzipan has set, brush the top and side(s) of the cake with a little cooled, boiled water, then roll out the gum paste as above and cover the cake.

(a)

(b)

(c)

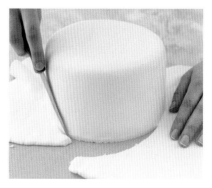

Covering Cake Boards with Gum Paste

FOR 1 DRUM
powdered sugar, for dusting
gum paste

YOU WILL NEED
pastry brush
cake board
rolling pin
¼in. marzipan spacers
    (optional)
icing smoother
sharp knife
scriber or sharp needle
piece of ribbon, about ⅜in. wide
    and long enough to fit around
    the edge of the cake board
double-sided tape or a glue stick

Whenever you need to cover a cake board in gum paste, simply follow the method below using the quantities specified by a particular recipe or by using the chart opposite. If you are new to covering cakes, start with slightly more gum paste than specified so you have plenty of gum paste to work with.

1 Using the pastry brush, lightly brush the top of the cake board with cold water **(a)**. Dust the work surface with a little powdered sugar, then knead the gum paste until it is soft and pliable. Roll out the gum paste until it is ¼in. thick, using marzipan spacers, if you like **(b)**.

2 Carefully lift the rolled gum paste and gently drape it over the top of the cake board **(c)**, taking care not to stretch or pull it. Use your hands to smooth it over the top of the drum, making sure to smooth out any air bubbles. For a flat, smooth finish, smooth the top of the gum paste again with the icing smoother **(d)**. Trim off any excess gum paste with the sharp knife **(e).** Use the scriber to prick out any remaining air bubbles in the gum paste.

3 Wrap the ribbon around the edge of the cake board **(f)**, securing the join at the back with double-sided tape and trimming as necessary.

(a)   **(b)**   **(c)**

(d)   **(e)**   **(f)**

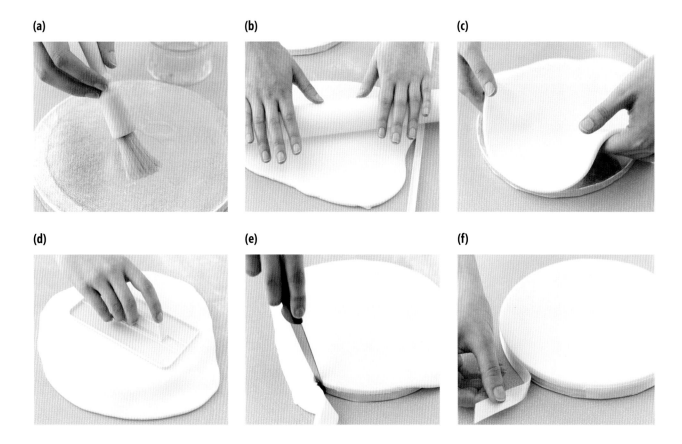

Covering Cakes and Cake Boards

Whenever you need to cover a cake board in gum paste; cover a cake in gum paste or marzipan; or cover a cake or cupcake with buttercream or chocolate ganache, simply follow the methods on pages 152–154 and use the quantity of gum paste, marzipan or buttercream or ganache specified by the charts below.

Gum paste quantities for covering cake boards	
Cake board	**Gum paste**
4in.	6oz.
5in.	7oz.
6in.	10½oz.
7in.	14oz.
8in.	1lb. 4oz.
9in.	1lb. 8oz.
10in.	1lb. 10oz.

Gum paste/marzipan quantities for covering cakes	
Cake	**Gum paste/ marzipan**
4in.	14oz.
5in.	1lb. 2oz.
6in.	1lb. 5oz.
7in.	1lb. 10oz.
8in.	1lb. 14oz.
9in.	2lb. 4oz.
10in.	2lb. 12oz.

Buttercream and chocolate ganache quantities for covering cakes and cupcakes	
Cake	**Buttercream/ chocolate ganache**
4in.	¾ cup
5in.	1 heaped cup
6in.	1¼ cup
7in.	2 cups
8in.	2¼ cup
9in.	3¼ cups
10in.	4½ cups
12 cupcakes/24 mini cupcakes	1½ cups

Stacking Tiered Cakes

2 or more cake tiers of different sizes, covered with gum paste and attached to cake boards the same size as the cakes
stiff-peak Royal Icing (see page 46)

YOU WILL NEED
doweling guide (see page 171)
scriber or sharp needle
plastic dowel rods (4 for each tier except the top one)
pen with edible ink
strong scissors
small angled metal spatula
large angled metal spatula
2 icing smoothers
carpenter's level (optional)

HINTS
Cakes covered in gum paste should be allowed to dry overnight, uncovered, in a cool, dry place before they are stacked.

If the dowel rods are hollow, cut them to size with strong scissors. If the dowel rods are solid, score them at the correct length, with a craft knife, then snap them.

1 Place the bottom tier on the work surface and position the doweling guide on top of the cake. Using the doweling guide, select the position of the dowel rods according to the size of the following tier, then mark the position of the first four dowel rods by lightly pricking the top of the cake with the scriber **(a)**. When selecting the position of the dowel rods, bear in mind that they need to be placed inside the diameter of the following tier to hide them from view.

2 Push the dowel rods straight down into the cake until they are resting on the cake board **(b)**. Using the pen with edible ink, mark each dowel rod at the point where it protrudes from the top of the cake—the mark should be level with the top of the cake. Remove the marked dowel rods from the cake then line them up on the work surface and assess the average height of the marked lines. Using the strong scissors, cut down each dowel rod to the average height, then push them back into the cake.

3 Using the small angled metal spatula, spread a thin layer of royal icing over the area between the dowel rods **(c)**—the royal icing will anchor the following tier in place. Using the large angled metal spatula to help you, carefully place the following tier on top of the dowel rods **(d)**. Move the tier into the center with icing smoothers. Ensure the top tier is level, using the carpenter's level, if you like. Leave the cake 10 minutes to allow the icing to set. Repeat for further tiers as necessary.

(a)   **(b)**

(c)   **(d)**

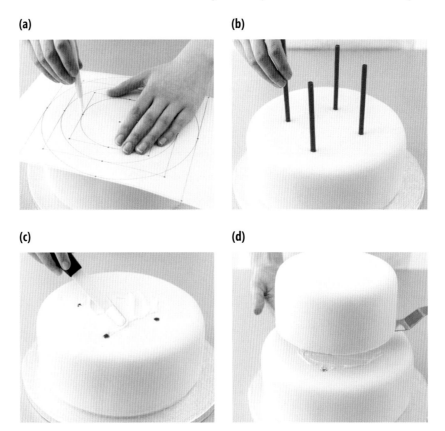

Piping Hints and Techniques

PREPARING TO PIPE

stiff- or soft-peak Royal Icing
    (see page 46) or Frosting
    (see page 118)

YOU WILL NEED
tip (optional)
pastry bag

HINT
If the icing tip does not sit comfortably on the end of the bag the icing will be pushed out of the gap between the tip and the bag and you will not be able to pipe effectively.

1 Select a tip and attach it to the pastry bag. If you are using a disposable pastry bag, snip off the end before inserting the tip. To attach a small tip, gradually snip off the end of the pastry bag until about half of the tip protrudes comfortably from the end of the bag. To fit a large tip, gradually snip off the end of the pastry bag until the end of the tip protrudes comfortably from the end of the bag.

2 Fill the pastry bag with icing or frosting, taking care never to fill it more than about one-third full. Using the back of your hand, ease the filling toward the tip, expelling any air in the bag as you do so. Fold the top corners of the bag toward the center to stop the icing from escaping. Fold the top of the bag toward the tip, then fold again to secure. Hold the bag in your dominant hand, then lightly place two fingers from your nondominant hand near the base of the tip to steady the bag.

PIPING FROSTING SWIRLS

Frosting (see page 118)

YOU WILL NEED
large plain, open-star or
    closed-star (not shown) tip
large heavy-duty pastry bag

Select a tip and attach it to the pastry bag, then prepare to pipe as above.

High Swirls add extra height to cupcakes. They are often used to decorate cupcakes and feature in most of the cupcake recipes in this book. To pipe a high swirl, hold the pastry bag vertically, then, starting at the edge of the cupcake, pipe the frosting in a fluid spiral motion toward the center, slightly overlapping the frosting as you work—this will give the swirl height.

Flat Swirls produce a lovely roselike effect, as you'll find in the Rose Swirl Cupcakes recipe (see page 22). To pipe a flat swirl, hold the bag vertically, then starting at the center of the cupcake, pipe the frosting in a fluid spiral motion toward the edge, taking care not to overlap the frosting.

High Swirl, piped with
a large plain tip

High Swirl, piped with
a large open-star tip

Flat Swirl, piped with
a large open-star tip

MAKING A DISPOSABLE PASTRY BAG

Disposable pastry bags are widely available and come in a variety of sizes, but it's also easy to make your own out of parchment paper.

YOU WILL NEED
parchment paper
ruler
scissors

HINT
Homemade pastry bags are great for piping royal icing, but piping intricate details requires a tip for this level of decoration so store-bought bags are best.

1 Cut a 12 x 12in. square of parchment paper. Fold the square in half diagonally and make a firm crease. Cut along the crease to make two triangles in total.

2 Take one of the parchment triangles, and place it on the work surface with the longest side farthest away from you. Take the top left-hand point in your right hand and curl it under until it touches the bottom point—the parchment should form a cone during this process **(a)**. Hold the two points firmly together in your left hand **(b)**. With your right hand, curl the top right-hand point **(c)** over the top of the existing cone until all the points meet and a definite cone shape has formed.

3 Holding the points between your thumb and forefingers, gently shuffle the position of the points until you form a very sharp point at the end of the cone.

4 Fold the triangle formed at the sharp end of the cone toward the tip, then fold again to secure **(d)**. The bag is now ready to be filled with stiff- or soft-peak royal icing. Snip off the end before use.

(a)   **(b)**

(c)   **(d)**

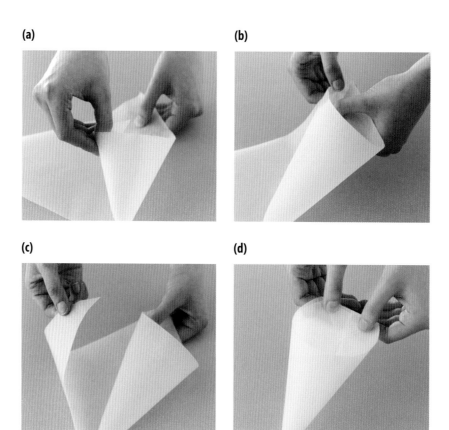

PIPING ROYAL ICING

Thanks to its incredibly versatile nature, royal icing is used for a range of decorating techniques, from icing cookies and piping intricate details to securing gum-paste decorations and building gingerbread houses. Depending on its purpose, it is made up to one of three consistencies: stiff-peak, soft-peak and flood-consistency (see page 46). Stiff- and soft-peak consistencies should be spooned into a pastry bag before use. (Flood-consistency royal icing should be transferred to a plastic squeeze bottle before using.)

Select a small tip and insert it into a pastry bag, or simply snip the end off of a disposable bag.

Piping Intricate Dots, Tear Drops and Lines

soft-peak Royal Icing (see page 46)

YOU WILL NEED
pastry bag with a small tip attached
small paintbrush (optional)

HINT
If you are decorating a cake, you may find it easier placing the cake on a tiltable turntable, tilted away from you when piping details onto the side(s) of the cake.

Following the instructions on page 157, fill a pastry bag with soft-peak royal icing and prepare to pipe.

Dots—hold the pastry bag at a right angle to the surface of your cake or cookie. Holding the tip about 1/16in. away from the surface, gently squeeze a small amount of icing out of the bag to form a dot, then carefully lift the tip away. The more you squeeze the bag, the bigger the dot will be. If a peak forms on top of the dot, flatten it with a small, dampened paintbrush.

Tear Drops—create a dot as above, then drag the tip through the top of the dot to create a tear-drop shape.

Lines—with the pointed end of the tip touching the surface of your cake or cookie, gently squeeze the icing out of the bag, then lift the bag slightly away from the surface and pipe a line, applying a slow, even pressure to the bag as you do so. To end the line, bring the pointed end of the tip back to the surface, then gently pull it away.

Stiff-Peak Royal Icing

Soft-Peak Royal Icing

Flood-Consistency Royal Icing

Gum Paste, Flower Paste and Modeling Paste

These three forms of rolled fondant can be used in many different ways to decorate cakes and cookies. Of the three types, gum paste is the most widely available and most commonly used, but all three can be bought at specialist sugarcraft stores and online, though I prefer to make my own modeling paste.

GUM PASTE

This sweet rolled fondant is used as a final covering for cakes and cake boards and can also be formed into simple decorations such as plain leaves and flowers. Widely available and easy to use, gum paste is pliable, rolls out well and dries with a lovely smooth, slightly shiny, surface.

FLOWER PASTE

Flower paste (also known as "petal paste" or "florist paste"), is a more pliable form of gum paste. You can roll it out more thinly than gum paste without the risk of it tearing and it also dries much harder. It's readily available from specialist suppliers (see page 172) and is mainly used in much smaller quantities for detailed decorations that require delicate molding, such as the roses for the Rose Cupcakes (see page 126) and the Magnificent Mini Cakes (see page 121), and the ribbon detail for the Orange Pomander Cake (see page 94).

MODELING PASTE

Adding sodium carboxymethylcellulose (CMC) to gum paste creates an icing known as modeling paste, which is stronger than gum paste. Modeling paste takes longer to dry than gum paste, but it also dries much harder, making it good for cakes requiring larger sugarcraft decorations, such as the corsages for the Ivory Corsage Wedding Cake on page 114, the teddy bears and rabbits for the Baby Shower Cupcakes on page 110 and the handle and spout for the Teapot Cake on page 122.

Making Modeling Paste

To make modeling paste, sprinkle 1 teaspoon of CMC straight onto the work surface and then knead 12oz. gum paste into it and transfer to an airtight container. The gum paste will start to thicken immediately, and will continue to do so over a period of 24 hours.

Using Gum Paste, Flower Paste and Modeling Paste

• Before rolling or molding gum, flower or modeling paste, dust the work surface with a little powdered sugar. Knead gum and modeling pastes until they are soft and pliable. Knead flower paste until it is smooth and elastic, pulling it apart to soften it if necessary.

• White gum, flower or modeling paste can be colored with food coloring pastes. To color, simply spread a small amount of food coloring paste onto the gum, flower or modeling paste using the end of a toothpick, and knead until combined. Repeat until the desired color is achieved.

• Once exposed to the air, gum, flower and modeling pastes will gradually harden. If you are working in batches or delicately molding a small amount of paste, store the remaining paste in an airtight container until needed to prevent it from drying out and cracking.

Rolling out Gum Paste, Flower Paste and Modeling Paste

• When a recipe states to roll out gum, flower or modeling paste "very thinly," roll out the kneaded paste until it is about $\frac{1}{16}$in. thick.

• When a recipe states to roll out the gum, flower or modeling paste "quite thinly," roll out the kneaded paste until it is about $\frac{1}{16}$–$\frac{1}{8}$in. thick.

• When a recipe states to roll out the gum, flower or modeling paste until it is $\frac{1}{4}$in. thick, you will find that marzipan spacers are extremely useful for achieving an accurate thickness.

Designs, Guides and Templates

To use the templates, trace the outline of the template onto thin cardboard, then carefully cut it out with a pair of scissors. To use the designs, simply trace each one onto a sheet of paper or thin cardboard. To download printable versions visit www.dbp.co.uk/icingonthecake

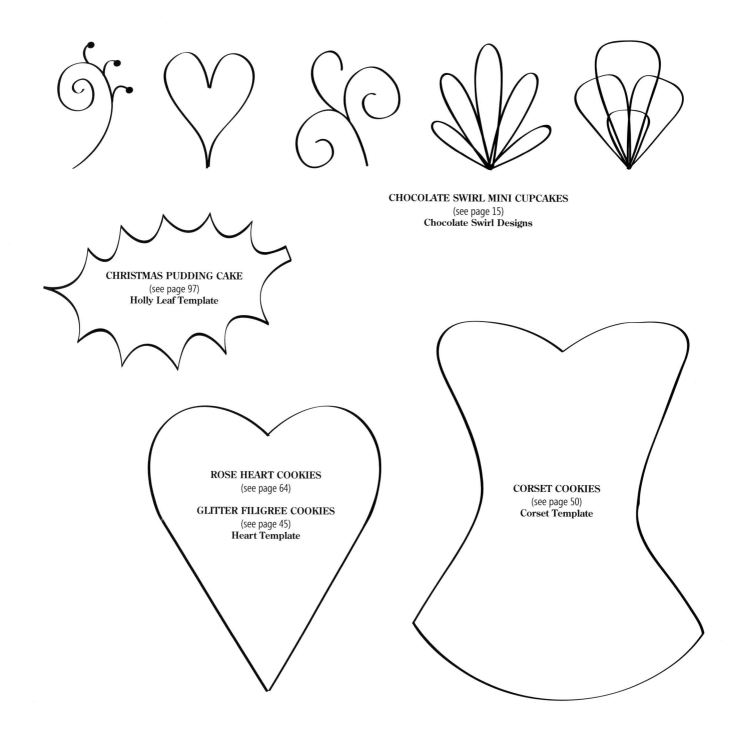

CHOCOLATE SWIRL MINI CUPCAKES
(see page 15)
Chocolate Swirl Designs

CHRISTMAS PUDDING CAKE
(see page 97)
Holly Leaf Template

ROSE HEART COOKIES
(see page 64)

GLITTER FILIGREE COOKIES
(see page 45)
Heart Template

CORSET COOKIES
(see page 50)
Corset Template

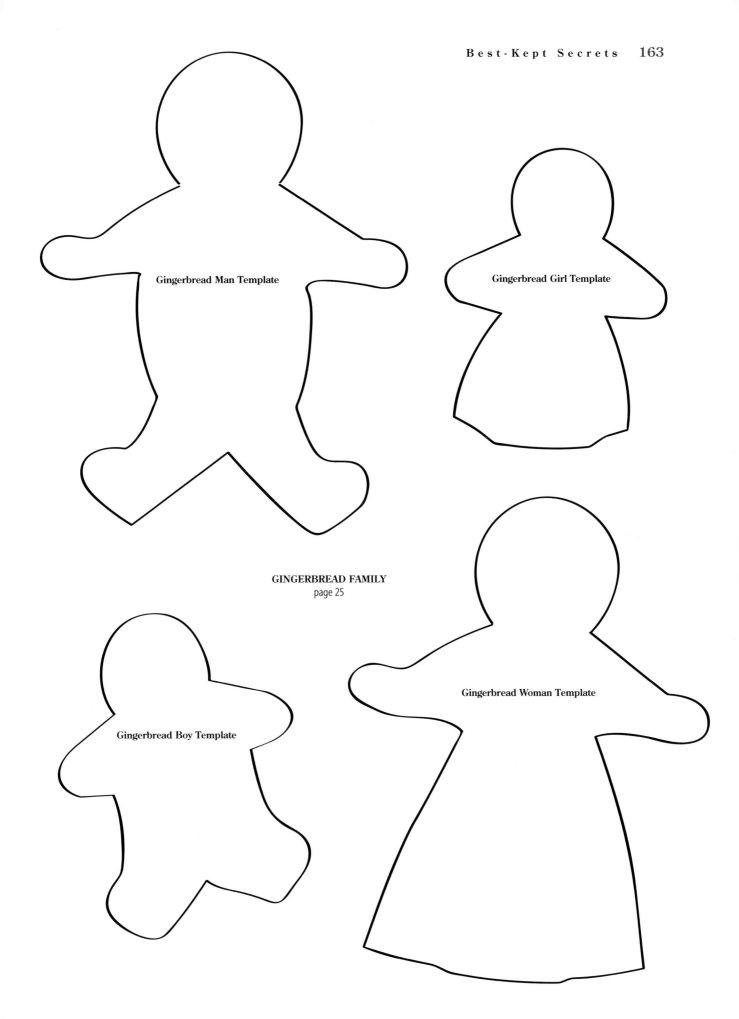

Gingerbread Man Template

Gingerbread Girl Template

GINGERBREAD FAMILY
page 25

Gingerbread Boy Template

Gingerbread Woman Template

To use the templates, trace the outline of the template onto thin cardboard, then carefully cut it out with a pair of scissors. To download printable versions visit www.dbp.co.uk/icingonthecake

DRAGON CAKE
(see page 74)

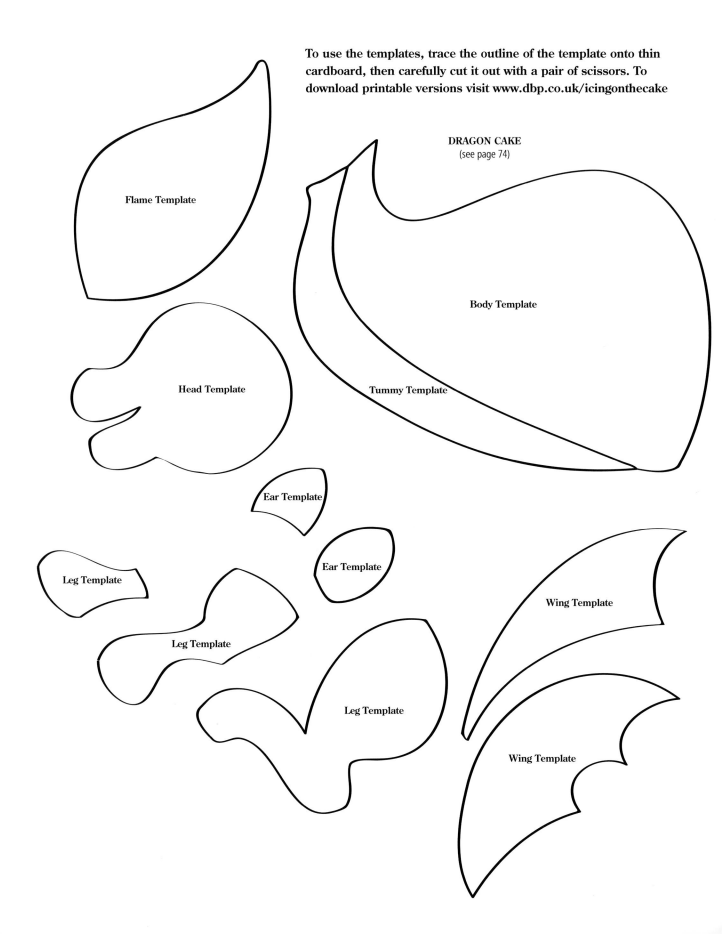

Flame Template

Body Template

Head Template

Tummy Template

Ear Template

Ear Template

Wing Template

Leg Template

Leg Template

Leg Template

Wing Template

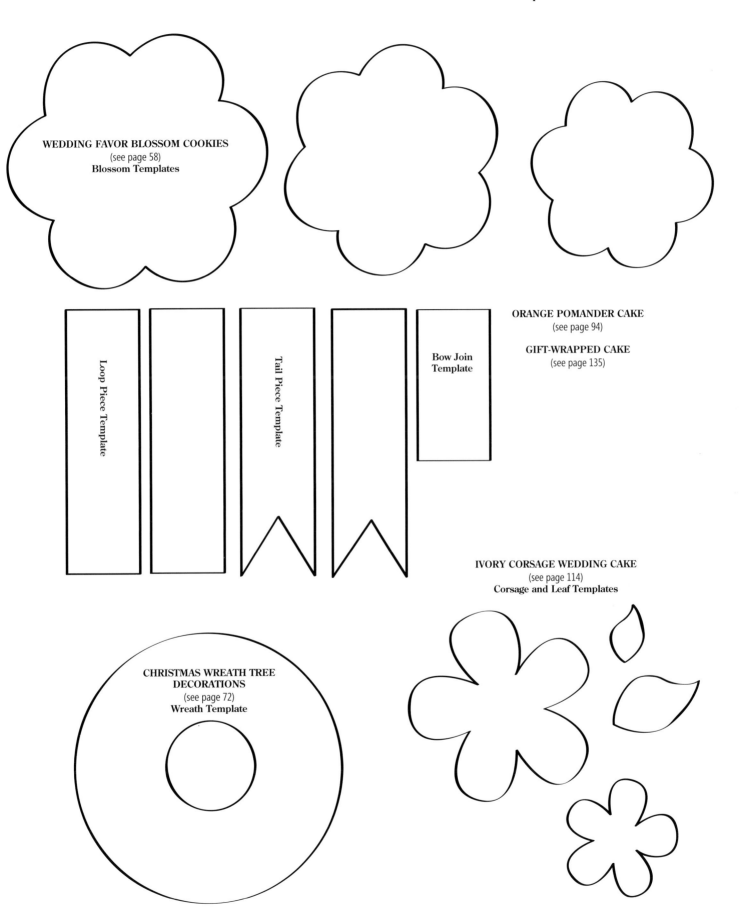

WEDDING FAVOR BLOSSOM COOKIES
(see page 58)
Blossom Templates

Loop Piece Template

Tail Piece Template

Bow Join Template

ORANGE POMANDER CAKE
(see page 94)

GIFT-WRAPPED CAKE
(see page 135)

IVORY CORSAGE WEDDING CAKE
(see page 114)
Corsage and Leaf Templates

CHRISTMAS WREATH TREE DECORATIONS
(see page 72)
Wreath Template

To use the templates, trace the outline of the template onto thin cardboard, then carefully cut it out with a pair of scissors. To use the designs, simply trace each one onto a sheet of paper or thin cardboard. To download printable versions visit www.dbp.co.uk/icingonthecake

Roof Panel Template

Side Wall Template

GINGERBREAD HOUSE
(see page 78)

Heart Template

End Wall Template

Door Template

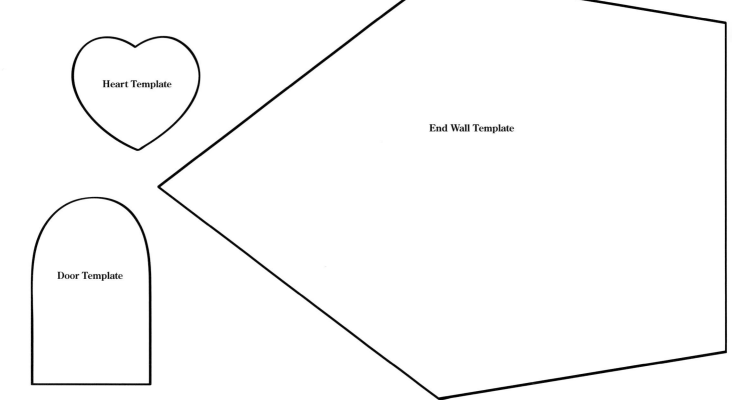

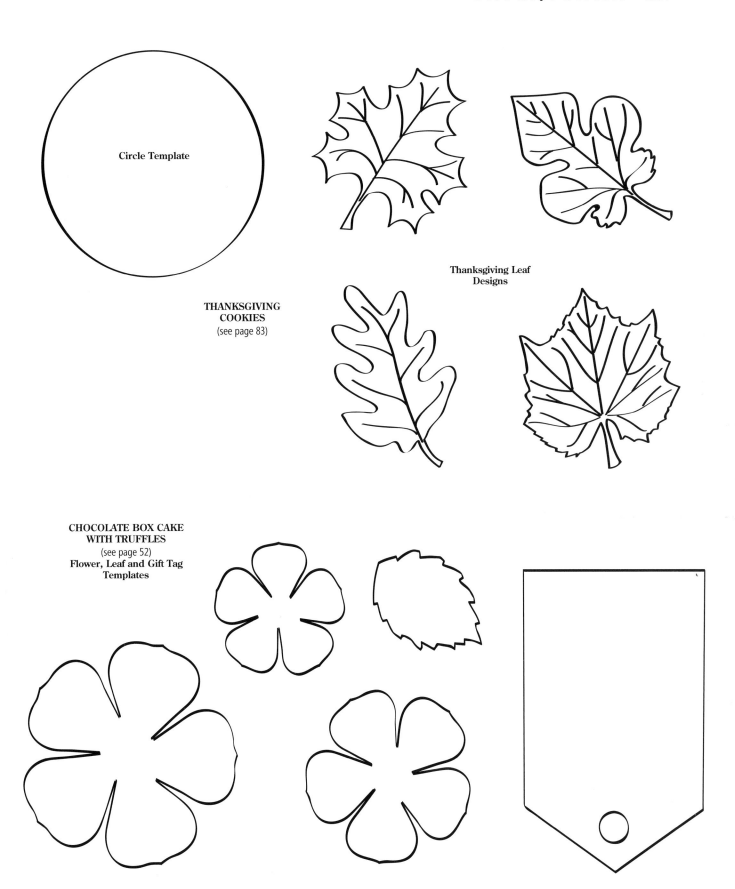

Circle Template

**THANKSGIVING
COOKIES**
(see page 83)

**Thanksgiving Leaf
Designs**

**CHOCOLATE BOX CAKE
WITH TRUFFLES**
(see page 52)
**Flower, Leaf and Gift Tag
Templates**

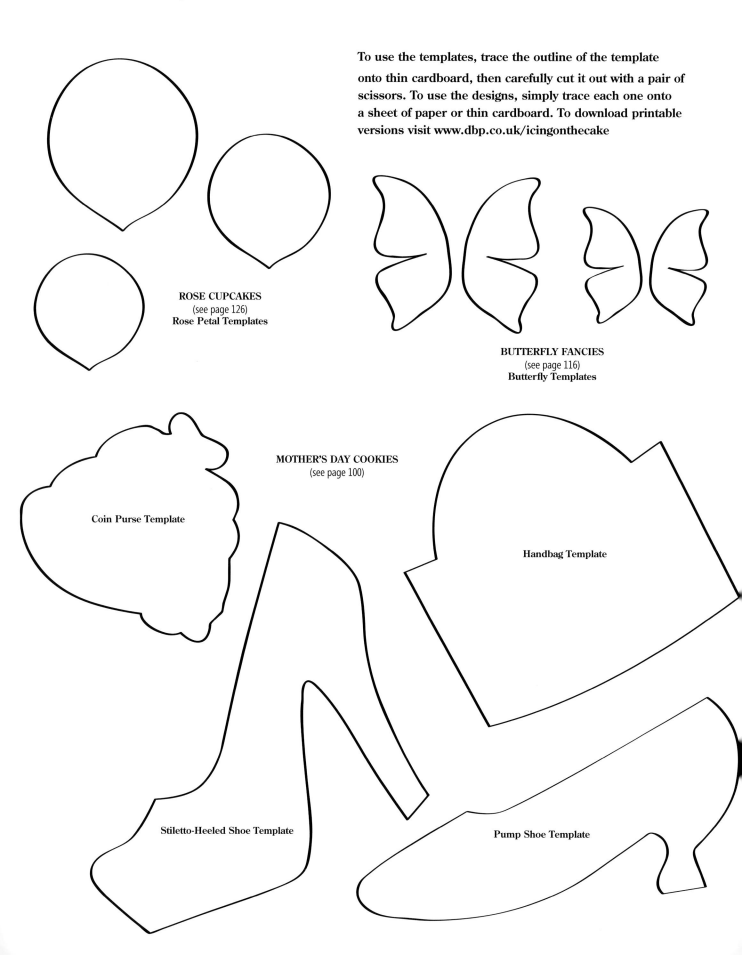

To use the templates, trace the outline of the template onto thin cardboard, then carefully cut it out with a pair of scissors. To use the designs, simply trace each one onto a sheet of paper or thin cardboard. To download printable versions visit www.dbp.co.uk/icingonthecake

ROSE CUPCAKES
(see page 126)
Rose Petal Templates

BUTTERFLY FANCIES
(see page 116)
Butterfly Templates

MOTHER'S DAY COOKIES
(see page 100)

Coin Purse Template

Handbag Template

Stiletto-Heeled Shoe Template

Pump Shoe Template

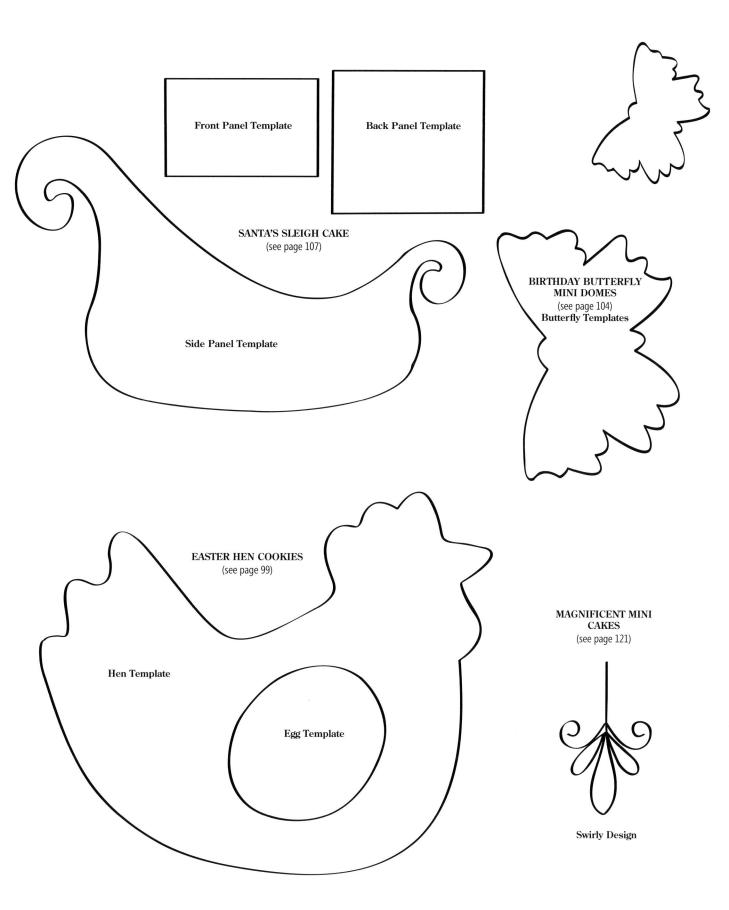

Front Panel Template

Back Panel Template

SANTA'S SLEIGH CAKE
(see page 107)

BIRTHDAY BUTTERFLY MINI DOMES
(see page 104)
Butterfly Templates

Side Panel Template

EASTER HEN COOKIES
(see page 99)

MAGNIFICENT MINI CAKES
(see page 121)

Hen Template

Egg Template

Swirly Design

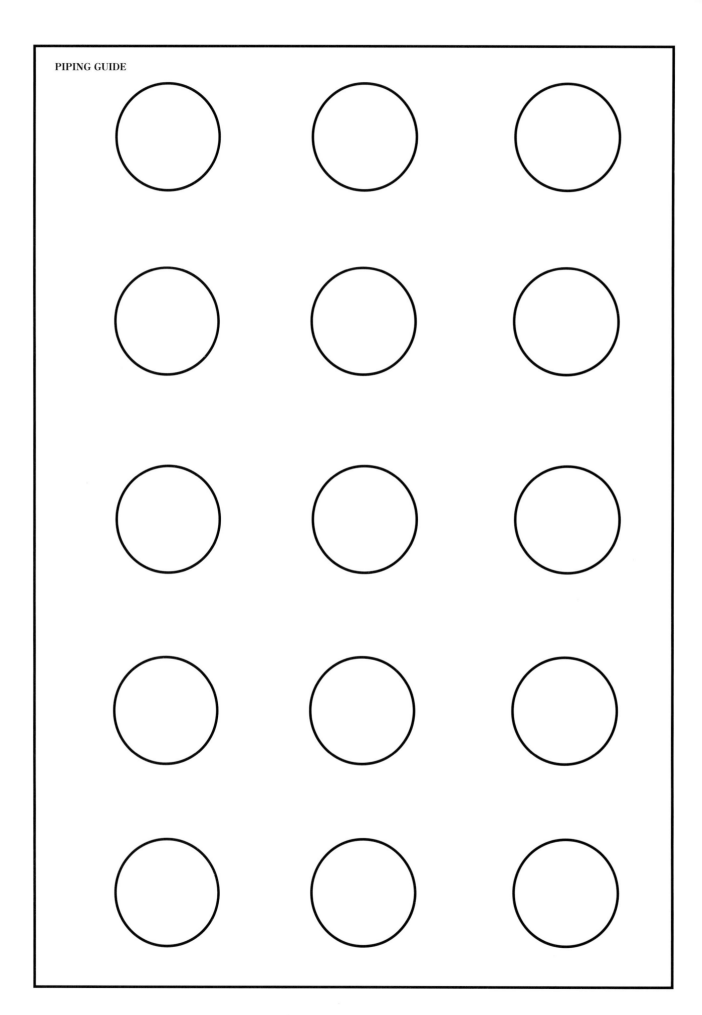

To use these guides, simply trace each one onto
a sheet of paper or thin cardboard. To download
printable versions visit www.dbp.co.uk/icingonthecake

DOWELING GUIDE

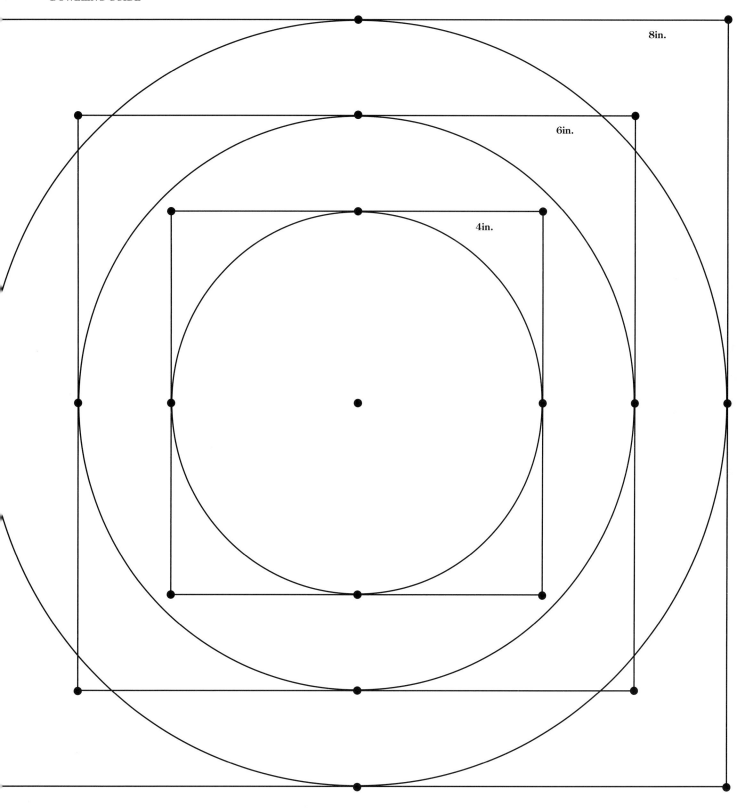

8in.

6in.

4in.

Suppliers

GLOBAL SUGAR ART
www.globalsugarart.com
Global Sugar Art, LLC
625 Route 3, Unit 3
Plattsburgh, NY 12901
tel: (toll free) 800-420-6088
Online supplier of a comprehensive
selection of more than 10,000 high-quality
cake and confectionery decorating products,
including unique items for the beginner to
the expert decorator.

GOLDA'S KITCHEN
www.goldaskitchen.com
Online supplier ships baking and
measuring equipment, specialty cake
decorating, chocolate and confectionery
supplies, and kitchen tools, knives and
appliances to the USA and worldwide.
Golda's Kitchen Inc.
2885 Argentia Rd Unit 6
Mississauga, ON Canada L5N 8G6
toll free 1-866-GOLDA-99

SUGARCRAFT™
www.sugarcraft.com
Online baking catalog. Suppliers of hard-to-
find baking tools, ingredients and supplies
for creative decorators.

WILTON
http://www.wilton.com/store-locator/
Shop using the online store for high-quality
cake decorating equipment and tools and
all the cake decorating accessories you
need. Or, enter your zip/postal code (USA
and Canada only) or the city and state/
province and the distance you are willing to
travel to find Wilton stores that offer Wilton
classes (stores that teach Wilton classes
offer the largest range of Wilton products).

Index

Acknowledgments

What an adventure my first book has been and I have loved every minute of it. A mixture of fun and creativity—with a lot of hard work added in! I hope it will inspire you to try things that perhaps you thought you'd never be able to do.

My thanks to Grace Cheetham at Duncan Baird Publishers for giving me the opportunity to publish this book and for her encouragement and support; to Manisha Patel for her design talents and endless patience; to Krissy Mallett for her wonderful editing skills and bubbling enthusiasm (not to mention her fair hands as my "stunt double"); and to Alison Bolus and Georgine Waller who made sense of my initial text over hundreds of emails. Thank you also to my photographer, Jon Whitaker, for making it a very happy shoot and for his beautiful photographs; to Jon's assistants Thea, Ben and Simon; and to Lucy Harvey for her stylish props—many of which I wanted to take home to use myself!

Over the last year I have, on occasions, been somewhat elusive in the family home, and so a huge thanks goes to my husband, Colin, and our sons, Sam and Ben, for their love and understanding while I wrote this book. Thanks too to the rest of my family—my Mum, Valerie, and Dad, John Miller, my sister, Leigh Miller, brother, James Miller and his wife, Michelle, for all their help and input. Thanks also to friends in the village, Laura Carter and Sarah Jones, who were there at the beginning, and to Martha Allfrey, for her encouragement and inspiration (particularly when it came to the brownie recipe). And thanks to all those who have helped along the way: Polly Hawkins, Jemma Morgan, Annie Meston, Emily Van Eesteren and Sara Broome to name but a few.

Thank you all... x